CHINESE COOKING
MADE EASY

COMPILED BY DOUGLAS MARSLAND

MURDOCH BOOKS®

Sydney • London • Vancouver • New York

CONTENTS

DISCOVER THE DELIGHTS OF
CHINESE CUISINE

Discover the delights of Chinese cuisine with food that's so easy to prepare and cook. Chinese cooking is famous for its variety, its subtle tastes, and its beautifully built-in balance of foods.

Chinese cooking is one of the world's great cuisines, popular in many countries around the world. Superb combinations of flavours and textures also offer the bonus of good health. It has been described as the ideal diet for our modern times, being high in protein and complex carbohydrates and low in calories. It also caters for vegetarians and people on a low cholesterol diet. Meat plays a secondary role and vegetables, particularly the non-starchy varieties, predominate.
Grains are plentiful, mainly rice and wheat. Rice is grown in the south and forms the staple diet. It is also used for noodle making and flour. Wheat is grown in the north and north-west, and used for flour and many varieties of noodles, which are served in place of rice.

Meats used are low in fat and high protein foods are important. For hundreds of years soy beans have been used for their rich protein, which closely resembles that of meat. During preparation, the beans are ground and mixed with water, converting them into a milky substance, then into a curd and finally a thick junket-like substance is formed, sometimes

called bean curd cheese. It can be dried, deep-fried, salted, made into sauces, steamed or eaten fresh. Soy bean sprouts are also eaten as a vegetable.

Sweets are seldom eaten. The Chinese prefer savoury foods. Between-meal snacks include many delicious dumplings, steamed buns and dim sum. Fresh fruit is usually served at the end of a family meal. The few desserts that are available are usually reserved for banquets.

The format of a family meal is simple. Every dish is served on the table at the same time, not in courses as in the West.

Most modern food markets have pork, chicken and beef shredded or cut into chunks, as well as a variety of marinated meats and poultry. Chinese foodstores sell freshly roasted and barbecued pork and cooked ducks and chickens, whole and in portions. By slicing, dicing and freezing before use, they are always available for quick meals.

Many ingredients, such as water chestnuts and lychees, are available in cans, and a great variety of ready-made sauces can be found on the shelves of most supermarkets and Asian foodstores.

CHINESE COOKING CLASS

Chinese cooking is easy when you know how. In the following pages, we look at cooking utensils and how to use them, and the basic methods of cooking Chinese-style. The rest is a little practice, a little experimenting, and lots of visits to Chinese restaurants to compare results.

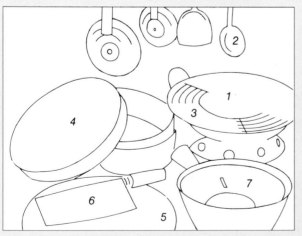

1 *Wok*
2 *Charn (stirring ladle)*
3 *Strainer*
4 *Steamer*
5 *Chopping board*
6 *Cleaver*
7 *Clay pot*

BASIC KITCHEN UTENSILS

We all have our own favourite knives, pots and pans for cooking, and these can be used with great success for Chinese cooking. In a Chinese kitchen, the utensils are very few but practical, namely the wok, wok charn, cleavers, strainers and chopsticks.

The wok is a thin metal all purpose cooking pan, with high sides and rounded bottom. It can be used for stir-frying, deep-frying, parboiling, simmering, braising, boiling and steaming. By placing a set of steaming baskets into the wok, a first class steamer is made, which will enable as many as five different dishes to be cooked at the one time e.g. fish, dim sum, egg rolls, chicken or duck, rice and sponges. The wok is also ideal for omelettes and for outdoor cooking.

The wok charn is designed to fit the curvature of the wok. It is used mainly for stir-fry dishes, to turn food and prevent burning, or sticking.

Light and heavy cleavers are both made from tempered steel; the light cleaver is used for slicing meat and vegetables and the heavy is used for chopping through bones, crab and lobster shells. The reverse edge is used for mashing and when held upright, the handle serves as a grinder for spices and black beans.

The flat edges are used for transferring chopped food from the board to serving plates, pounding and tenderising meats, crushing ginger and garlic and, when combined with the light cleaver, forms an excellent mincer.

Strainers are used for removing deep-fried foods from hot oil, draining off excess oil and in the making of potato and noodle baskets.

Chopsticks come in various sizes, with an extra long size to be used in the kitchen suitable for beating eggs, adding and removing food from a deep-fryer, turning food while cooking, adding beaten egg to soups, forming egg flower patterns, and removing ingredients from jars.

Optional extras include *steam boats* for Mongolian hot pot, small *cooking baskets* for steam boat cookery and a *tong hock* for measuring and transferring liquids.

CHINESE METHODS OF COOKING

The main styles of cooking are: stir-frying, steaming, deep-frying and roasting, all with a minimum of fuel, which in former days was a matter of necessity. In early days wood, coal and charcoal were used. Today all these forms of cooking are carried out with modern gas and electric ranges, electric woks and microwave ovens, still with consideration towards economy.

STIR-FRYING This technique is used for tender cuts of pork and beef, poultry, sea- food and vegetables. The ingredients are sliced, shredded, diced or minced, then stir-fried in a wok using a wok charn. Cook over high heat in the minimum of oil. This method seals in the natural juices and preserves colour, texture and flavour.

Gas is preferred for Chinese cooking for the instant control of temperature. If using an electric stove, flat-bottomed woks are available from most Chinese foodstores.

Ingredients are added to the wok in order of texture and cooking time. The preparation of ingredients and being well organised is the key to success for Chinese cooking:

1	Dried mushrooms	8	Baby or mini corn
2	White radish	9	Fresh coriander
3	Garlic	10	Chillies
4	Fresh ginger root	11	Lotus root
5	Shallots	12	Capsicum (pepper)
6	Bean sprouts	13	Tangerine
7	Snow peas (mangetout)		

❖ Collect all ingredients required for the recipe. Allow time for soaking dried ingredients like Chinese mushrooms.

❖ Slice meat, poultry and seafood. Arrange in order of cooking on a kitchen tray. Prepare marinades if required, and marinate. This can take up to 30 minutes.

❖ Wash, drain and cut vegetables to size. Parboil or blanch if necessary.

❖ Measure liquid ingredients like oil, sauces, stock and seasonings. Blend any thickening agent with stock or water and stir before adding to wok. Chop ginger, garlic and chillies. Arrange ingredients in the order that they will be added to the wok for cooking.

❖ Collect cooking utensils and warm serving dishes.

This basic preparation should be done for all recipes before any style

Stir-frying: prepare vegetables in advance.

Heat oil in a wok until very hot. Fry garlic and ginger first to flavour oil.

Add larger, denser vegetables and pour in sauce or stock.

of Chinese cooking is started as it makes Chinese cooking easy. Confucius once said, "Cooked Chinese food waits not for any man". It should be served and eaten at once, to experience the best flavour, texture and colour of the food.

DEEP-FRYING The deep-frying technique is used extensively throughout Chinese cuisine, from hors d'oeuvres to main course dishes and desserts. You can use a great variety of ingredients, such as pork, beef, poultry, seafood, vegetables, various types of noodles, skins for wrapping as well as fruit.

Deep-frying ingredients are cut into even-sized pieces and dipped into a protective coating of batter, such as seasoned flour, beaten egg and breadcrumbs, spring roll or wonton skins, even cellophane paper can be used to protect ingredients. Then they are immersed in hot oil to cover, until cooked.

Oil or lard should be heated to 180°C (350°F) in a deep-fryer or deep-sided saucepan, not more than half full.

If a saucepan is used without a thermometer, a slice of fresh ginger root can be added to indicate the oil's temperature. When the ginger is golden, the oil is right for deep-frying.

On reaching 180°C (350°F) oil or lard will cease to bubble, and a faint blue haze will start to rise.

Tips for optimum deep-frying results include:

❖ Ingredients can be marinated then drained before dipping into batter and being fried.

❖ Ingredients can be two-thirds cooked, then drained. Just prior to serving, oil can be reheated to the correct temperature, and the final stage of deep-frying completed. This gives even cooking and a crisp texture. This method is called double-frying.

❖ Only add small quantities of ingredients to the oil at one time. This maintains the oil's temperature and prevents absorption.

❖ Drain food thoroughly and serve with prepared dips or sauces.

❖ Allow oil to cool then strain. Store covered to prevent dust from settling on the surface.

Add a quantity of fresh oil to used oil before re-using; this prevents oil from discolouring and gives a higher smoke point when reheating.

ROASTING Roasting in China originally took place outdoors on large spits or used hanging hooks over open fires.

The Chinese style of roasting can be done in the modern stove by making wire hooks and hanging, from the top shelf of the oven, marinated duck, chicken or strips of pork brushed with barbecue sauce, with a roasting dish containing several centimetres of water placed underneath to catch the drips.

Roasting can also be done by placing a cake rack over a roasting pan containing 2 to 5 cm of water, and placing the meats onto the rack. Meat should not sit flat in a roasting dish stewing in its own juices as it tends to become tough.

Roasting starts on a high heat and is later reduced to medium. Baste during cooking with marinades or honey and warm water.

STEAMING Cooking by the steaming method enables three to five preparations to be cooked at the one time, over the minimum of fuel. Chinese steaming baskets are made from bamboo and consist of two baskets and a lid. They come in various sizes, and extra baskets can be purchased individually. A new bamboo steamer should be soaked in water overnight, before using the first time. Chinese metal steamers are also available. They have two baskets with a lid and a boiler-style base, and can be used for direct and indirect steaming. The base and lid can serve as a boiler, or be used for stewing long-cooking ingredients.

DIRECT STEAMING Bamboo steamers are placed into a wok containing several centimetres of vigorously boiling water. Food to be steamed can be placed on a heatproof plate or tray, or on banana leaves cut to basket size, Chinese cabbage or lettuce leaves. Always leave enough room for the steam to circulate around the food and cook it by direct contact. Place a clean cloth over the top basket before putting the lid on. This will absorb condensation and prevent it from dripping onto the steamed products.

Many varieties of yum cha dumplings, dim sum, gow gees, savoury custards, pork and fish balls and spare ribs are steamed; as well as whole fish and poultry, meat dishes, vegetables, cakes and puddings.

Steaming time varies with different foods. Dumplings and dim sum take 20 minutes, a whole fish weighing 750 g will cook in 15 minutes, sponges and cakes cook in 30 minutes, while medium-sized chickens and larger cuts of pork take 40 minutes. The longer cooking items are placed in the lower baskets and other baskets are placed on top in order of cooking times.

INDIRECT STEAMING   This is usually done in a heatproof basin, which can be covered with aluminium foil. The basin is placed in a large saucepan or boiler with its ingredients. Boiling water is added to surround the basin to about half its height. Then the saucepan lid is added. The water must remain boiling during the cooking time. Check water level when steaming. Extra boiling water should be added if necessary for both methods of steaming.

Food cooked by indirect steaming includes: whole ducks, whole chickens, slow-cooked stewed meats and savoury custards. It is also an effective method for reheating rice. Steamed food is best slightly undercooked, as it continues cooking in its own stored heat after being removed from the steamer.

SIMMER COOKING   This gentle method of cooking is used for soups and long cooking of less tender cuts of meat. It is also suitable for seafoods to avoid over cooking. A stock or sauce is brought to the boil with the ingredients added, then simmered over a low heat until tender.

PARBOILING   Parboiling is used when cooking ingredients of different textures. The tougher varieties are added to boiling stock or water for a short time. They are then refreshed in iced water to set colour and prevent overcooking. The cooking time, when tender ingredients are added, will then be the same.

CHINESE FIRE POT COOKING   The Chinese fire pot is a example of simmer cooking. It enables a larger number of diners to be catered for and to participate in the cooking, which is done at the table.

Fire pots or steam boats as they are also called are made from a variety of metals. Individual wire baskets or chopsticks are used to cook the food in small quantities, in simmering stock. Hot coals or heat beads are placed into the chimney in the centre of the cooking container. This keeps the stock simmering. An electric frying pan can substitute for the fire pot.

The fire pot is placed in the centre of the dining table on a heatproof tray or on a cutting board covered with aluminium foil. Boiling stock is poured into the container, and the raw ingredients and condiments are placed around the pot.

Each diner selects and cooks food which is dipped into various sauces or raw egg. Steamed rice and Chinese tea are served with the meal, which can last several hours.

A fire pot or steam boat is used to cook dishes such as Mongolian Hot Pot

GLOSSARY

ABALONE (DRIED, FRESH OR CANNED)
Sometimes called mutton fish, it is a large mollusc used in soups, stir-fried dishes and salads. Slice fresh abalone thinly. Abalone only needs to be heated through. It will toughen if overheated.

AGAR AGAR A variety of dried seaweed which resembles vermicelli noodles. It must be soaked before use and can be used to replace gelatine. Available dried in powder and stick shape.

ANISE, STAR ANISEED Used for spice flavouring, when braising meats and poultry. Available dried, shaped like an eight pointed star.

BAMBOO SHOOTS Young shoots of the bamboo, cut when just appearing above ground. Available in various sized cans, whole, sliced or braised. Use as a vegetable or in combination dishes.

BEAN CURD A bland junket-like product made from white soy beans. Available fresh, in long-life packs, canned and dried and the texture can be firm or soft. Firm textured curd is suitable for braising, deep-frying, in soups, steaming or stir-frying with other ingredients. Soft-textured curd can be used in various fillings or soups, or eaten fresh with a dip sauce. Bean curd can be blanched then refreshed before eating fresh. The dried form requires soaking in warm water before using in soups and as a wrapper.

BEAN PASTE, RED Red beans are cooked in water with sugar, then pureed.

Available canned in various sizes and used as a filling in steamed buns, pastries and puddings.

BEANS SPROUTS These are the sprouts of mung peas. They sprout within a few days and can be grown indoors throughout the year. The texture is crisp and the taste delicate. They are cooked briefly in stir-fried dishes and used in salads, soups and vegetable combinations. They are readily available fresh or canned.

BEAN SPROUTS, SOY Soy bean sprouts are larger than mung pea sprouts and have a slightly stronger flavour. Blanch in boiling water for 1 minute and refresh in cold water, if using in salads. Can be used to replace mung bean sprouts.

BEANS, BLACK These fermented small black soy beans are strongly flavoured. Use in suggested amounts with garlic and ginger in braised dishes, sauces, stir-fried beef, pork, chicken and seafood. Black beans are available both in cans and dried in packets of various sizes. The dried variety are inclined to become salty – store in a jar in a cupboard on opening packet, do not refrigerate. The canned variety is much milder in flavour, due to the canning process. Soak dried variety in warm water or sherry before using to reduce the salty flavour.

BEANS, YELLOW These fermented soy beans are actually light brown. When mashed, they can be stir-fried with garlic and ginger to form a sauce base for chicken, pork and

seafood. They are much milder in flavour than black beans. Ready-made sauce is also available canned.

BIRDS NESTS These famous ingredients are actually the nests of seaside swallows. Nests are made from small fish, seaweed and marine plants, which the swallow collects and pulls apart then mixes with saliva to form a nest, which is very gelatinous and rich in protein and vitamins. As the nest becomes very dry and hard, it must be soaked and boiled for several hours before using. Three grades are available: the most expensive are the whole nests, then broken nests and last, the small nest fragments. Birds nest soup is served at formal banquets and is considered a delicacy. All grades are sold by weight.

BITTER MELON (BALSAM PEAR) A green, shiny, wrinkled-skinned vegetable, shaped like a small cucumber. The flavour is cool and slightly bitter due to the quinine content. This is a popular summer vegetable sold fresh and canned. The melon can be seeded, filled with a minced filling and steamed. Use in soups or stir-fry with black beans, pork, chicken or seafood.

BLACK GLUTINOUS RICE Mainly used in sweet dishes, although its colour, when cooked, adds contrast to vegetables and protein. The cooking time and water absorption is similar to brown rice. When cooked, the rice has a very fragrant aroma and is deep purple to black in colour.

BROCCOLI, CHINESE (GAI LARN) This variety has more leaves and less flowers than European broccoli. It is sold in bunches and can be stir-fried as a vegetable or combined with meats and seafood. Avoid overcooking to preserve the deep fresh green colour.

CABBAGE (GAI CHOY) This has a jade green stalk with darker green leaves and is a compact small cabbage with a slight mustard flavour. Cut into 2 to 5 cm pieces and use in clear soups.

CABBAGE, CELERY (WONG AH BARK) This variety has long, white, wide stalks, tightly packed with crinkled green leaves. Used in soup, braised or blanched for cabbage rolls.

CHINESE CABBAGE (BARK CHOY) This cabbage has long white stems and green leaves. Use in stir-fried dishes. The white and green are cut into 2 to 5 cm pieces. The white is stir-fried first in a little oil with ginger, then the green leaf is added with salt and sugar and 2 tablespoons stock. Cook covered for a few minutes until bright green and crispy tender.

MUSTARD CABBAGE (CHOY SUM) This is a smaller vegetable than bark choy with similar uses. The stalk and green are cut into 5 cm sections, then blanched and served with oyster sauce. It is a popular restaurant dish. Leaves and stalks are separated for cooking, then cut into sections. The stalk is stir-fried first in a little oil and ginger, then the leaf is added with stock, sugar and salt, and quickly steamed, covered.

CHESTNUT, WATER This root of a marsh plant resembles a small gladioli bulb. It is often grown as a second crop around the edges of rice fields, as both foods grow in muddy conditions. The chestnut has a crisp, delicate flavour which is similar to apples. The black skin must be peeled off before use and the flesh sliced, diced or minced. Eat raw in salads or include in steamed, deep-fried or stir-fried preparations to

give a crisp texture. Chestnuts are available fresh, and whole or sliced in cans.

CHILLIES Used fresh or dried to season dishes cooked in the Szechuan style.

DATES, RED Red dates are used in soups, braised dishes and desserts. They are soaked in warm liquid to plump them before cooking. Sold in packets.

DRAGON EYES (LONGAN) Similar to lychee fruit only smaller. Use in sweet and sour sauces, fruit salad, or appetiser cocktails. Available fresh in season and canned in syrup.

EGG, SALTED DUCK The fresh duck eggs are soaked in a salt brine for 40 days. They must be cooked before eating. Either boiled or steamed on top of rice, salted eggs can be used for omelette, braised whole, steamed with pork or used for salty egg cake.

FISH, DRIED SALTED Various sized fish are dried and salted, either whole or

in fillets. Slice thinly, place onto a small plate, add 1 to 2 tablespoons of vegetable oil and some shredded ginger. Place on top of rice after water is absorbed and steam 20 minutes. Eat with rice.

FISH MAW This is the dried and deep-fried stomach lining of fish. Must be soaked before use. Has no fish flavour when cooked. Used in soup and pork dishes. The large curved crisp pieces are sold by weight.

FIVE SPICE POWDER A combination of star anise, cloves, fennel, cinnamon and anise, used in marinades for roasting pork and poultry. Use sparingly in braises, some batters and to flavour breadcrumbs for coating. Sold in small jars and packets.

FUNGUS, DRIED BLACK OR WHITE The black variety is called chee yee and, when soaked, can be used in place of mushrooms and when cooking soups, stir-fry or simmered and added to salads. The white variety is cooked in a syrup and served as a dessert called "white cloud".

GINGER ROOT Fresh green ginger root is used extensively in Chinese cooking. It can be pickled, crystallised or preserved in syrup. The dried, ground variety should not be used as a substitute for fresh when cooking Chinese food. Available fresh, or chopped and sliced in jars.

GINKO NUTS Available in cans for instant use in soups, vegetarian dishes and some puddings.

GLUTINOUS FLOUR Made from glutinous rice and ground, this flour is used for pastries and dough products.

GLUTINOUS RICE (NOR MU) Available white and black. The white comes in whole grain form and in packs of flour. Use in desserts, pastries, and various dumplings with sweet and savoury fillings. When cooked, it is very sticky and is also known as sticky rice throughout Asia.

GOLDEN NEEDLES The dried buds of the tiger lily. When soaked these are used in vegetarian and poultry dishes.

HOISIN SAUCE Also called Peking or barbecue sauce. This thick brownish-red sauce is made from soy beans, spices, garlic and chilli. It complements most cooking ingredients – spare ribs, pork, poultry and seafood. It can also be used as a table condiment or a base for dip sauces.

LOTUS LEAVES The leaves from the water lily plant, available fresh and dried. The fresh leaves are used sparingly, sliced in various dishes to impart flavour and fragrance. Dried leaves are soaked before use and are used for wrapping rice, meat and sweet fillings e.g. sweet bean paste, before steaming.

LOTUS ROOT The starchy root of the lotus flower, about 5 cm in diameter. When sliced, reveals an attractive pattern of holes running through the length of the root. Used mainly for soups and in braised dishes. When dried, soaking is required before cooking. Available fresh and canned.

LOTUS SEED PASTE Available in cans, this paste is used as a filling for sweet buns, moon cakes and puddings. The young seed of the water lily can be eaten raw as a fruit or boiled, mashed and sweetened as with the red beans. The seeds are also used in soups, with braised duck, or can be crystallised.

LYCHEE (LICHEE) Grows on a tree in tropical areas. It resembles a round red strawberry with a thin shell-like skin. It has white translucent flesh and one black seed. Sweet and delicate in flavour, it is available fresh and canned. Used as a dessert with ice cream, in sweet poultry and pork dishes or sweet and sour sauce.

MIXED SPICE Finely ground spice combination, including allspice, nutmeg and cinnamon; used to flavour cakes and buns.

MUSHROOMS, CHINESE Choose the thick black variety. Soak in warm stock or water for 20 minutes to soften. Retain stalk for stock pot. Chinese mushrooms retain their shape in cooking. Can be stir-fried, braised, steamed, chopped and added to rice and poultry stuffings. Store in airtight jar.

NOODLES, DRIED Dried thin and thick noodles are made from wheat and rice flour, with and without eggs. They are usually cooked in boiling water before frying. Some varieties of rice noodles are soaked in warm water then stir-fried or added to soups. Flavoured noodles are popular and cook quickly e.g. prawn, chicken, beef and curry flavours are available.

NOODLES, FRESH Fresh egg and eggless wheat noodles are available in most Chinese supermarkets. Thin, round and flat as well as spaghetti size are made daily. They can be frozen in recipe size amounts. Fresh rice noodles flavoured with prawns or parsley as well as plain, are available in sheets and strips ready for boiling.

OLIVE NUTS These are the kernels of the Chinese olive and their texture is softer than other nuts used in cooking. They are best toasted to a light ivory colour and can be used as a garnish or with mild flavoured dishes. They are approximately 14 mm in length.

Oyster sauce Made from fresh oysters, this sauce is used as a flavouring in cooking or served as a table condiment. Available in bottles and cans, it is best to refrigerate after opening.

Parsley, chinese (coriander) Fresh coriander has a wonderful aroma when crushed or chopped. It can be used fresh, cooked with other ingredients or used as a garnish. Sold fresh in bunches.

Pickles, chinese A combination of ginger, turnip, carrot and cucumber in a pickle syrup. Sold in jars.

Red beans Small red beans similar in size to mung beans. When cooked, mashed and sweetened the red bean paste is used in sweet buns, desserts, and puddings. The beans are also available in powder form.

Red ginger Fresh young ginger, peeled, sliced and cooked in a sugar syrup. Available in jars or cans.

Rice Rice is the staple food of southern China. White short-grain is preferred, although brown rice is used in rural areas. Both white and brown rice are available with long and short grains.

Sausages, chinese, pork or liver Chinese sausages are sold in pairs or pre-packaged packs. The pork variety is a light pink waxed colour; the liver variety is dark. They are both steamed by direct method or on top of rice, before eating or adding to other ingredients. Both varieties are savoury.

Sesame oil Made from sesame seeds, this oil tastes very strong, so use sparingly. Adds flavour to dip sauces, salads, soups, and is rarely used as a cooking oil.

Sesame paste, ground Toasted sesame seeds, with a peanut butter texture. Used in sauces and available in cans and jars.

Sharks fin Used in thick rich soups, omelettes and in poultry stuffings. It is high in calcium and protein and comes in cans and dried.

Soy sauce Essential in Chinese cooking to flavour pork, beef, poultry and fish. Available in dark form for cooking and light form for a table condiment. Salt-reduced soy sauce is also available.

Spring roll skins Available fresh or frozen in large and small sizes. Fresh skins can be re-wrapped and frozen in smaller quantities.

Vegetarian mock duck Made from wheat flour, gluten, safflower oil, soy bean extract, sugar, salt and water. Sold in 285 g cans. It is a light food which can replace duck in most recipes.

Wonton skins A thin fresh pastry made from eggs and flour. Sold by weight fresh or frozen. Skins are 8 cm square. Fillings can be made from fresh raw ingredients such as pork, beef, seafood, poultry or vegetables. They can be deep-fried, steamed, boiled or baked. They can be re-wrapped and frozen.

Wheat starch Wheat starch is little used in food preparation but is extensively used as a thickening agent. Flour has less thickening power and makes a more opaque gel than cornflour. Its characteristic flavour is preferred by many to that of other thickening agents. It is sold in smaller packets in Chinese food stores.

YUM CHA
AND OTHER APPETISERS

This section includes recipes which will tantalise the tastebuds without spoiling your appetite for the main meal to come. Small portions and light quick cooking are the secret.

Yum cha recipes can form a meal in themselves. They are a series of little snacks, either steamed or fried, and are normally eaten at midday as a kind of brunch. This is a meal to be eaten with a few friends as the point is to have as big a selection as possible. The range of choice is enormous as dim sum are made from several kinds of flours, eggs, bean curd, yams, bread dough and pastry. These are wrapped around minced meat fillings and covered with different kinds of wrappings and skins. Tea is the proper drink to have with this snack meal - the teapot should be refilled as soon as it is empty.

To serve at home, provide a selection of dipping sauces such as chilli, soy, red vinegar, sesame oil and garlic paste which should be put in the centre of the table.

Fried Pork Patties (page 21), Chicken and Ham Rolls (page 14) and Lychee Appetiser (page 14)

PEARL BALLS

1 cup (185 g) glutinous rice, soaked in cold water 1 hour

500 g boneless pork with a little fat, minced

2 teaspoons ginger wine

2 tablespoons light soy sauce

1 egg, beaten

1 tablespoon cornflour

1 spring onion, finely chopped

½ teaspoon sugar

½ teaspoon salt

¼ teaspoon white pepper

1 Drain rice. Combine pork with remaining ingredients. Form into 20 balls with wet hands. Roll each ball in rice until well coated. Arrange on two heatproof plates. Leave 1.5 cm space between each ball for rice expansion.

2 Steam covered in a double boiler over high heat for 1 hour. Serve with prepared mustard, soy sauce or chilli dip.

SERVES 4

❖ **CANNED LYCHEES**

If using canned lychees, retain lychee juice for sauces or fruit punch.

PRAWN AND PORK DIM SUM

24 wonton skins

FILLING

200 g green (uncooked) prawns, shelled

250 g lean pork mince

3 tablespoons pork fat, minced

3 Chinese mushrooms, soaked in warm water 20 minutes

75 g bamboo shoots, diced, or ½ carrot, shredded

SEASONINGS

2 teaspoons oyster sauce

1 teaspoon salt

2 teaspoons sugar

2 teaspoons light soy sauce

½ teaspoon sesame oil

¼ teaspoon pepper

1 teaspoon cornflour

3 tablespoons water

1 teaspoon bicarbonate of soda

1 Wash and devein prawns and pat dry. Dice and put into mixing bowl. Add mince and pork fat, mushrooms without stalks and bamboo shoots. Pound until firm. Add seasonings and pound again until seasonings are well mixed.

2 Put 2 teaspoons of filling in each wonton skin. Use one hand to hold and shape into a column. Using a knife, flatten on top.

3 Put dim sum in a greased steamer or on a plate. Steam over high heat for 10 minutes.

MAKES 24

❖ **POUNDING**

Pounding is done by throwing the mixture into the bowl; this gives the mixture a lighter texture with a slight chew.

LYCHEE APPETISER

565 g can lychee fruit, drained

1 tablespoon salted cashews, finely chopped

75 g crabmeat, canned or freshly cooked

1 tablespoon mayonnaise

1 teaspoon light soy sauce

1 spring onion, finely cut

2 teaspoons lemon juice, strained

red ginger or capsicum (pepper), for garnish

shredded lettuce

1 Combine cashews, crabmeat, mayonnaise, light soy sauce, spring onion and lemon juice. Pack into lychee fruit.

2 Top each with a thin slice of red ginger or capsicum (pepper). Arrange on finely shredded lettuce and serve chilled.

SERVES 6 TO 8

CHICKEN AND HAM ROLLS

2 whole chicken breasts

1 slice square ham steak cut 1 cm thick

chicken seasonings

2 teaspoons hoisin sauce

½ cup (60g) plain flour

¼ teaspoon salt

1 egg, beaten

½ cup milk (125 ml) or use half water and half milk

1 tablespoon cornflour

1½ cups (375 ml) oil, for deep-frying

30 g vermicelli noodles, deep fried

1 Remove skin and bone chicken breasts. Place each breast and the small underfillets on a board and cover with foil. Using a rolling pin, press out each chicken piece thinly. Partly cover each breast with the fillet to make an even size. Sprinkle with chicken seasoning.

2 Cut ham into four 1 cm wide strips. Spread each strip with hoisin sauce. Place each piece of ham diagonally onto each chicken breast. Roll up and secure with two toothpicks. Chill 15 minutes.

3 Sieve flour and salt. Blend in egg and milk to form batter. Sprinkle rolls with cornflour then coat with batter. Deep-fry two at a time in hot oil until golden. Remove toothpicks and serve sliced and garnished with fried noodles.

SERVES 4

❖ **PREPARATION TIME**

Chinese cooking requires more preparation time than cooking time. Many dishes can actually be cooked in less than 10 minutes. To reduce the preparation time, many convenient ingredients are now available from Chinese foodstores and supermarkets. Rice, which is available in conventional white or brown, long- or short-grain, can now be replaced by the quick-cooking variety in both white and brown, saving 50 per cent of the cooking time.

Pearl Balls (page 14) and Bacon-wrapped Water Chestnuts (page 17)

STEP-BY-STEP TECHNIQUES

1 *To make spring rolls, you can either use the triangle method (see spring rolls recipe) or place prepared filling on one side of spring roll wrapper and roll short side over, tucking underneath filling.*

2 *Fold both sides of wrapper in towards the centre.*

3 *Roll up, dampening remaining corner with a little flour and water to seal.*

4 *Deep-fry rolls in a pan or wok, and allow to drain before serving*

SPRING ROLLS

15 large sheets spring roll pastry, cut diagonally to make triangles

3 Chinese mushrooms, soaked in warm water for 20 minutes, or fresh mushrooms

1 chicken breast fillet, minced

100 g pork mince

oil, for frying

200 g water chestnuts, finely chopped

150 g bamboo shoots

100 g Chinese barbecued pork (char sui) or ham, diced

1 small carrot, finely chopped

2 tablespoons plain flour mixed with 1½ tablespoons water

sweet and sour sauce, to serve

SEASONINGS

2 tablespoons oyster sauce

1 teaspoon salt

2 teaspoons sugar

2 teaspoons light soy sauce

1 teaspoon wine

¼ teaspoon pepper

¼ teaspoon sesame oil

3½ teaspoons cornflour mixed with 3 teaspoons water

❖ **HINT**

Marinate foods overnight for tenderness and flavour.

1 Steam mushrooms, remove stalks and finely chop caps. Marinate chicken and pork with 3 teaspoons combined seasonings for 10 minutes and set aside. Heat oil in a pan, sauté water chestnuts and bamboo shoots and set aside.

2 Heat another pan with oil and pour in marinated meat and Chinese barbecued pork to sauté. Add mushrooms, carrot, water chestnuts and seasonings. Mix well with combined cornflour and water and let cool completely before wrapping in pastry.

3 Put each pastry triangle flat on table, place 1½ tablespoons of filling in centre of pastry and bring the two corners to opposite ends and roll. Use flour and water solution to seal.

4 Pour oil in a heated pan, put spring rolls in hot oil to deep-fry until golden brown. Serve with sweet and sour sauce.

MAKES 30

CHINESE SAUSAGE ROLLS

PASTRY

350 g plain flour

2 teaspoons baking powder

½ cup (125 g) sugar

1 tablespoon butter

½ to ¾ cup (125 to 180 ml) warm water

½ teaspoon vinegar

FILLING

7 Chinese sausages, washed and halved

1 tablespoon oil

1½ teaspoons red bean paste

2 cm wedge brown sugar slice
or 6 teaspoons sugar

1 teaspoon oyster sauce

½ cup (125 ml) water

pinch salt

1 tablespoon plain flour

1 Sift flour and baking powder in a bowl. Add sugar and rub in butter. Use half the warm water to combine ingredients. Add a little bit more water gradually to work the flour into a dough and knead until smooth. Cover with a damp cloth and set aside for 1½ to 2 hours until doubled in size.

2 TO MAKE FILLING: Steam Chinese sausages for 7 minutes. Place oil in a pan to heat. Add red bean paste, sugar, oyster sauce, water and salt. Add flour to mixture and stir until lumps disappear. Add sausages and cool.

3 Roll the soft dough into a sausage-shaped roll. Divide into 14 portions. Press each into rectangular shape, 5 cm wide. Put sausage on one side of pastry and roll towards centre. Place on a rectangular piece of greaseproof paper, sealed edge facing down.

4 Place sausage rolls in a steamer and steam over high heat for 12 to 15 minutes.

MAKES 14

BACON-WRAPPED WATER CHESTNUTS

180 g canned whole water chestnuts

2 tablespoons hoisin sauce

4 to 6 rashers bacon, rind removed

1 Drain and dry chestnuts. Mix with hoisin sauce. Cut each bacon rasher into strips long enough to wrap around each chestnut. Secure with toothpick.

2 Arrange on a foil-covered tray. Roast at 225°C (430°F) for 10 to 15 minutes until bacon is crisp.

SERVES 6

❖ **HINT**

Place cooking ingredients on a tray in order of cooking. This can be done in advance, covered and refrigerated.

❖ **HINT**

Freeze fresh noodles, wonton skins and spring roll skins in recipe size amounts.

Spring Rolls (page 16), Chinese Sausage Rolls, Prawn and Pork Dim Sum (page 15)

For better results, cook rice the day before, or use leftover rice. Cook as quickly as possible, without burning.

BEEF AND SHALLOT FRIED RICE

20 g butter

450 g skirt steak, cut into very small dice

2 cups (400 g) cold cooked rice

salt and pepper

3 teaspoons soy sauce

2 teaspoons sugar

pinch pepper

3 spring onions, very finely chopped

1 Melt butter in a wok and stir-fry steak until it has changed colour.

2 Add rice and stir-fry over a high heat until rice is heated through. Add seasoning and serve decorated with finely chopped spring onions.

SERVES 4 TO 6

Silver Pin Noodles with Shredded Chicken and Beef and Shallot Fried Rice

SILVER PIN NOODLES WITH SHREDDED CHICKEN

NOODLES

1 cup (125 g) wheat starch

pinch salt

¾ cup (180 ml) boiling water

2 teaspoons oil

CHICKEN MIXTURE

1 chicken thigh fillet, sliced

½ teaspoon chopped fresh ginger root

½ teaspoon Chinese white wine or white wine

1 teaspoon cornflour

oil, for frying

1 Chinese mushroom, soaked in warm water for 20 minutes

1 spring onion, chopped

1 clove garlic

1 green capsicum (pepper), seeded and sliced

1 red capsicum (pepper), seeded and sliced

120 g bean sprouts

SEASONINGS

2 teaspoons oyster sauce

1 teaspoon sugar

2 teaspoons soy sauce

¼ teaspoon sesame oil

1 Sift wheat starch and salt in a mixing bowl. Pour in boiling water and stir. Cover for 5 minutes then remove and knead to form a smooth dough.

2 Roll out into a long sausage-shaped roll and cut into 24 equal portions. Knead each portion into the shape of a thin chopstick and cut again into 5 cm portions. Pinch ends to make them pointed. Put silver pin noodles on a greased plate to steam for 5 minutes. When cooked, coat with oil to prevent them from sticking together.

3 Marinate chicken for 20 minutes with ginger, Chinese white wine and cornflour. Shallow-fry in hot oil 5 minutes and set aside. Steam mushrooms, chop and set aside.

4 Heat pan and add more oil. Sauté briefly

spring onion, garlic and capsicum (pepper) then bean sprouts. Add chicken meat, silver pin noodles and mushrooms. Sauté together a few minutes, sprinkle with wine, add seasonings and serve hot.

SERVES 4 TO 6

PORK AND LETTUCE ROLLS

Generally, meat filling and lettuce leaves are served separately; guests fill and roll their own lettuce leaves

30 g dried Chinese mushrooms, soaked in warm water 20 minutes

45 g water chestnuts, finely chopped

60 g bamboo shoots, finely chopped

3 spring onions, finely chopped

200 g canned crab, drained and flaked

2 teaspoons oil

125 g minced pork

1 teaspoon sesame oil

2 teaspoons soy sauce

1 teaspoon oyster sauce

1 tablespoon sherry

1 lettuce, washed and dried

1 Drain mushrooms, remove stems and chop mushroom caps finely.

2 Heat oil in a wok and stir-fry pork until golden. Stir in mushrooms, water chestnuts, bamboo shoots, spring onions and crab. Cook 1 minute. Combine sesame oil, soy sauce, oyster sauce and sherry and stir.

3 Place 2 level tablespoons of the mixture into the centre of each lettuce leaf. Fold in the ends of the lettuce leaf and roll up to form a neat parcel.

SERVES 4

Pork and Lettuce Rolls

❖ NOODLES

Instant noodles are available both plain and flavoured with chicken, prawn, beef, curry or vegetables. They can be used in soups, or stir-fried with a topping. Their cooking time of 2 minutes has captured the noodle market. Dried noodles can be boiled then mixed with a small amount of oil and refrigerated in portion sizes several days before use.

STEAMED GOW GEES

FILLING

350 g green (uncooked) prawn meat or boneless white fish cut into 5 mm dice

60 g pork fat, finely chopped

60 g bamboo shoot, finely chopped

½ teaspoon salt

¼ teaspoon white pepper

½ teaspoon sesame oil

2 teaspoons cornflour

DOUGH

1½ cups (185 g) plain flour or Chinese gluten-free flour

1½ tablespoons lard

1½ cups (375 ml) boiling water

DIP SAUCE I

4 tablespoons light soy sauce

2 teaspoons white vinegar

¼ teaspoon sesame oil

DIP SAUCE II

2 tablespoons tomato sauce

1 tablespoon chilli sauce

1 Combine filling ingredients. Divide into 36 portions.

2 Sieve flour into a basin. Add lard and stir in boiling water with a knife to form dough. Let stand covered until cool.

3 Form dough into a sausage-shaped roll and cut into 36 even-sized pieces.

4 Roll each piece of dough into 5 cm circles on a lightly oiled surface. Place a portion of filling onto each round. Fold lower edges of dough over filling to form a half circle. Press edges firmly and pleat edge.

5 Arrange gow gees on two lightly greased plates, leaving enough space between each to prevent sticking. Steam in a double boiler for 10 to 15 minutes. Serve with dip /sauce

6 TO MAKE DIP SAUCE: Combine ingredients for the two sauces in two small bowls.

SERVES 4

CLOUD SWALLOWS

20 wonton skins

1 beaten egg white

oil, for deep-frying

FILLING

100 g chicken, finely chopped

100 g fish fillets, finely chopped

½ stalk celery, finely chopped

Steamed Gow Gees and Cloud Swallows

1 small spring onion, finely chopped

2 teaspoons light soy sauce

¼ teaspoon salt

SWEET AND SOUR SAUCE

¾ cup (180 ml) water

½ cup (125 g) sugar

½ cup (125 ml) white vinegar

1 tablespoon tomato sauce

1 tablespoon cornflour

1 Combine filling ingredients.

2 Place 1 teaspoon of mixture onto each wonton skin. Brush edges lightly with egg white. Fold to form a triangle. Place a dab of egg white on the left front corner of triangle. Join the front of the left to the back of the right side of triangle to form a swallow.

3 Deep-fry in oil to cover until golden. Serve with sweet and sour sauce.

4 TO MAKE SAUCE: Combine all ingredients in a saucepan. Beat and stir until boiling. Serve in bowls.

SERVES 4

FRIED PORK PATTIES

HOT WATER PASTRY

2½ cups (310 g) plain flour

¾ cup (180 ml) boiling water

¼ cup (60 ml) cold water (optional)

500 g pork, finely minced

½ teaspoon salt

pinch white pepper

2 tablespoons light soy sauce

½ teaspoon sesame oil

2 spring onions, finely chopped

2 to 3 tablespoons oil, for frying

DIP SAUCE

2 tablespoons vegetable oil

1 tablespoon light soy sauce

2 tablespoons white vinegar

1 teaspoon sugar

1 Sieve flour into a bowl. Stir in boiling water with a knife adding a little cold water if necessary to take up any excess flour. When cool, knead on lightly floured board until smooth. Cover with a basin and rest 30 minutes.

2 Combine pork, salt, pepper, soy sauce, sesame oil and spring onions. Chill 30 minutes.

3 Roll out dough with hands to form a sausage-shaped roll. Cut into 20 even portions. Lightly roll each portion into a ball. Roll out each ball into a 10 cm circle, with the edge thinner than the centre. The dough circles can be stacked with a piece of greaseproof paper between each. Cover with a basin to prevent drying out.

4 Divide pork into 20 portions. Place one in centre of each piece of dough. Bring the edges together to cover filling. Twist them slightly and pinch to seal.

5 Place seal side down onto board and reshape into a round patty. These may be made in advance and refrigerated.

6 Heat oil in a flat-bottomed pan. Reduce heat and fry patties 4 minutes on each side until brown. Serve hot with dip sauce.

7 TO MAKE SAUCE: warm oil in a saucepan, stir in soy sauce, vinegar and sugar to dissolve. Cool and serve in a small bowl.

SERVES 4 TO 6

❖ **HINT**

Toast sesame seeds in a dry pan and store in a jar. Keep a stock of oven-roasted nuts to use as a garnish.

SOUPS

There is an immense variety of soups in Chinese cooking,
some are light and clear and others are thick and filling. They may
be either bland and served to clear the palate, or spicy and pungent,
served as a contrast with other foods.

Most soups have a short cooking time, though some thick
and hearty soups, which have dried or salted ingredients added for
extra flavour, require a longer time.

Green vegetables are usually added in the last few minutes
so they will retain their crispness and bright colour. When tougher
vegetables like carrots are used, they are parboiled first and then added
with the more tender leafy vegetables.

Though some soups are eaten to begin the meal, they are also
served as a wonderful accompaniment to rice dishes. There are a number
of sweet soups in Chinese cooking which are served only at formal dinners
or banquets, and these are customarily eaten at the end of a meal.

Chicken Noodle Soup (page 24), Wonton Soup (page 26)
and Fish and Spinach Soup (page 24)

Both shredded ham and egg are frequently used to garnish soups and other dishes.

Ham garnish: Cut a thick slice of ham into shreds. The pieces are usually placed in the centre rather than being scattered over the top of the dish.

Egg garnish: Beat 1 egg briefly. Heat 1 teaspoon oil in a wok. Add egg and tilt the wok to form a layer of egg. Cook egg until set, roll up Swiss-roll style, and cut into slices. As with the ham garnish, the strips of egg are placed in the centre of the dish. Both ham and egg garnish may be diced.

CHICKEN NOODLE SOUP

250 g thin long life noodles

1 tablespoon light soy sauce

¼ teaspoon sesame oil

250 g chicken breast, cooked and cut in 5 cm strips

½ bunch fresh mustard cabbage, cut in 2 cm pieces

8 cups (2 litres) chicken stock

1 Cook noodles in 1 litre boiling salted water for 5 minutes; drain.

2 Place soy sauce and sesame oil in a large soup bowl. Top with cooked noodles. Arrange chicken and cabbage on top. Pour over boiling seasoned stock. Cover and let stand a few minutes before serving.

SERVES 6 TO 8

FISH AND SPINACH SOUP

250 g firm white fish fillets, cut in 2 cm x 1 cm slices

2 tablespoons seasoned cornflour

6 cups (1½ litres) fish stock

1½ tablespoons light soy sauce

1 tablespoon ginger wine

300 g spinach leaf, cut in 2 cm pieces

salt and pepper

1 Toss fish slices in cornflour to coat.

2 Bring stock to the boil. Add soy sauce, wine and fish pieces. Simmer covered for 6 minutes. Add spinach, cook uncovered until bright green, 1 to 2 minutes. Adjust seasonings and serve.

SERVES 6

BEAN CURD AND VEGETABLE SOUP

6 cups (1½ litres) vegetable stock

1 ripe tomato, skinned, seeded and cut in 1 cm dice

5 button mushrooms, sliced

60 g bean sprouts, root removed

125 g bean curd, sliced

salt and pepper

1 spring onion, finely chopped

1 Bring stock to the boil. Add tomato and mushrooms and simmer for 3 minutes. Add sprouts, bean curd and seasonings. Simmer covered for 2 minutes.

2 Serve with chopped spring onions.

SERVES 6

CRAB AND SWEET CORN SOUP

1 tablespoon vegetable oil

½ teaspoon chopped fresh ginger root

6 cups (1½ litres) fish stock, seasoned

1 tablespoon dry sherry

220 g crabmeat, flaked

125 g sweet corn

1 tablespoon cornflour blended with 2 tablespoons stock or water

2 egg whites, lightly beaten

chopped spring onions, to garnish

1 Heat oil in a wok. Add ginger and crabmeat, stir-fry 2 minutes. Add stock, sherry and sweet corn. When boiling, stir in blended cornflour and water to thicken. Remove from heat.

2 Pour in egg white in a thin stream. Garnish with spring onions.

VARIATION: Children love this soup, especially when chicken is used instead of crab. Simply substitute an equal quantity of chicken stock for fish stock, and chicken for crabmeat.

SERVES 6 TO 8

PEKING HOT SOUR SOUP

4 Chinese mushrooms, soaked in warm water 20 minutes

4 cups (1 litre) chicken stock

125 g lean pork, shredded

60 g canned bamboo shoots, shredded

125 g bean curd, cut in 1 cm dice

2 tablespoons white vinegar

1 tablespoon soy sauce

1 tablespoon cornflour blended with 4 tablespoons water

1 egg, beaten

½ teaspoon sesame oil

3 spring onions, chopped

1 Squeeze mushrooms dry and remove stems. Cut mushroom caps into thin strips.

2 Bring stock to the boil and add pork and mushrooms. Bring to the boil again, reduce heat and simmer for 8 to 10 minutes. Add bamboo shoots and bean curd and simmer for another 4 to 5 minutes.

3 Mix vinegar and soy sauce and stir into soup. Stir in blended cornflour and water and simmer, stirring constantly, until thickened.

4 Stir in beaten egg off the heat. Add sesame oil and spring onions and serve hot.

SERVES 4 TO 6

Peking Hot Sour Soup

STEP-BY-STEP TECHNIQUES

1 *To fold wontons: Place ½ teaspoon of filling in wrapper, fold in half and press sides together; fold in half again, pressing firmly at both sides of filling, but leaving corners open.*

2 *Bring two corners together, and cross over in front of filling; where they meet, brush lightly with water or beaten egg, to make them stick.*

WONTON SOUP

WONTONS

2 Chinese mushrooms, soaked in warm water 20 minutes

90 g lean minced pork

60 g prawn meat, minced

2 water chestnuts, very finely chopped

4 spring onions, very finely chopped

1 tablespoon soy sauce

2 teaspoons sherry

16 wonton wrappers

1 egg, lightly beaten

SOUP

1½ litres chicken stock

6 spring onions, white part only, thinly sliced

1 Squeeze mushrooms dry. Remove stalks and finely chop the caps. Combine mushrooms, pork, prawns, water chestnuts, spring onions, soy sauce and sherry. Stand 30 minutes.

2 Place ½ teaspoon of filling slightly off centre of each wrapper. Fold wrapper in half and press the edges together to seal them. Again, fold the wrapper in half. Pull the corners down into a crescent shape, overlapping the corners. Seal the overlap with a little beaten egg.

3 Drop the wontons one by one into boiling salted water and simmer 7 minutes, making sure they do not stick to the bottom of the pan. Drain the wontons. Bring chicken stock to the boil and add wontons and spring onions.

SERVES 6 TO 8

Wonton Soup

PORK AND PRAWN SOUP

350 g egg noodles, cooked

3 tablespoons oil

1 small onion, peeled and thinly sliced

2 slices fresh ginger root, finely chopped

250 g lean pork, finely shredded

50 g Chinese mushrooms, soaked in warm water 20 minutes and shredded

½ Chinese cabbage, shredded and blanched

100 g bean sprouts

125 g prawns

2 tablespoons soy sauce

1 litre beef or chicken stock

1 Heat oil in a wok. Add onion, ginger and pork and stir-fry for 2 minutes.

2 Add mushrooms, cabbage, bean sprouts and prawns; stir-fry for 2 minutes. Stir in soy sauce and stir-fry a further 1½ minutes. Remove from heat and keep warm.

3 Bring stock to the boil. Add half the pork mixture and bring to the boil again. Add noodles and heat through. Serve soup and top with remaining hot pork mixture.

SERVES 6

Pork and Prawn Soup

❖ **HINT**

Place cooking ingredients on a tray in order of cooking. This can be done in advance, covered and refrigerated.

SEAFOOD

The aim in cooking fish is to produce as natural a
flavour as possible from the freshest fish available. Steaming as well
as clear simmering are favourite ways of cooking fish because the subtle
natural flavour is retained and the flesh is both tender and moist.
However, deep frying, braising and even stir-frying are
methods which are also used.

Fish which is to be deep fried is either dredged in
flour or cornflour or is coated with a batter to seal in all of the juices. To
eliminate the 'fishy' taste, a number of seasonings can be used with the fish.
Ginger, garlic, spring onions, black beans, soy sauce and wine are the most
popular. The fish is often scored to permit the flavours to be absorbed
better and to expose a greater cooking surface.

Besides fish, the Chinese also eat a great deal of other seafood
including prawns, crab, lobster, scallops, clams and oysters. They are also
fond of sea cucumber, squid and sea urchins.

Though fresh seafood is generally preferable,
frozen seafood can be substituted successfully. Canned abalone
need only be heated very briefly.

Sizzling Mongolian Scallops and
Combination Seafood in Nests (page 30)

COMBINATION SEAFOOD IN NESTS

❖ **SQUID**

To prepare squid, remove the outer purple membrane. Place knife into tube and cut through at one edge. Open out tube. Lightly cut the inner surface to form a small diamond pattern. This acts as a tenderiser and enables the squid strips to curl when being stir-fried. Cut squid into 4 cm x 2 cm strips for cooking.

3 tablespoons vegetable oil

½ teaspoon salt

½ teaspoon chopped fresh ginger root

125 g scallops

125 g prepared squid cut into rings

125 g green (uncooked) prawns, shelled and deveined

125 g firm white fish, cut in 2½ cm dice

½ teaspoon chopped garlic

125 g broccoli florets

125 g snow peas (mangetout), stems removed

60 g Chinese cabbage, stems cut in 3 cm x 1 cm pieces

30 g bamboo shoots, sliced

30 g mini corn

15 g champignons, sliced

15 g straw mushrooms

1 tablespoon light soy sauce

2 tablespoons dry sherry

1 teaspoon sugar

pinch pepper

½ cup (125 ml) fish stock

2 tablespoons oyster sauce

1 tablespoon cornflour

3 tablespoons water or stock

1 Heat half the oil. Add salt and ginger, and stir-fry 30 seconds. Add seafood and cook 2 minutes. Remove from pan.

2 Heat remaining oil, add garlic, broccoli, snow peas (mangetout) and cabbage stems. Stir-fry 2 minutes. Add bamboo shoots, corn, champignons and straw mushrooms. Blend in soy sauce, sherry, sugar, pepper and stock.

3 Blend oyster sauce, cornflour and water. Bring sauce to the boil, and stir in cornflour mixture to thicken. Fold in seafood to reheat.

4 Serve in noodle nests.

SERVES 4

SIZZLING MONGOLIAN SCALLOPS

For this recipe you will need one sizzle plate, which consists of an iron plate that fits into a thick wooden mould of similar shape. Heat the iron plate on top of your stove for 5 minutes before adding cooked ingredients.

500 g scallops

1 tablespoon light soy sauce

1 tablespoon dry sherry

2 tablespoons vegetable oil

1 large onion, peeled and cut in eighths

1 teaspoon chopped fresh ginger root

SAUCE

1 teaspoon chilli garlic sauce

2 teaspoons hoisin sauce

1 teaspoon sesame oil

½ teaspoon five spice powder

1 teaspoon sugar

3 teaspoons peanut butter

3 tablespoons fish stock

1 In a bowl combine scallops, soy sauce and sherry. Heat oil in a wok. Add onion and stir-fry 1 minute. Add ginger, scallops and marinade, stir-fry 2 to 3 minutes.

2 Blend in sauce ingredients and stir-fry until boiling. Serve at once on hot sizzle plate.

SERVES 6

❖ **NOODLES**

Instant noodles are available both plain and flavoured with chicken, prawn, beef, curry or vegetables. They can be used in soups, or stir-fried with a topping. Their cooking time of 2 minutes has captured the noodle market. Dried noodles can be boiled then mixed with a small amount of oil and refrigerated in portion sizes several days before use.

STEP-BY-STEP TECHNIQUES

STIR-FRIED SQUID AND VEGETABLES

700 g squid

3 Chinese mushrooms soaked in warm water 20 minutes

1 bunch Chinese spinach or cabbage

3 tablespoons oil

1 onion

¼ teaspoon grated fresh ginger root

60 g bamboo shoots

100 g carrot, finely sliced

100 g green beans, finely chopped

100 g red or green capsicum (pepper), finely sliced

½ cup (125 ml) chicken stock

1 tablespoon soy sauce

2 teaspoons cornflour blended with 1 tablespoon water

1 Pull tentacles and intestines out of squid. Pull 'feather' out of body and discard. Cut tentacles from intestines, discard intestines. Rinse body and tentacles and peel skin from body. Drain well. Halve bodies lengthways and score the surface.

2 Discard mushroom stalks and slice caps.

3 Cut spinach into 5 cm strips. Parboil stalks for 3 minutes, drain and refresh under cold running water. Halve onion lengthways then cut into 4 lengthways strips. Separate into layers. Slice bamboo shoots.

4 Heat oil in a wok. Stir-fry squid 1 minute. Add onion and stir-fry for 30 seconds.

5 Add ginger, spinach, mushrooms, bamboo shoots, carrot, beans and red or green capsicum (pepper) and stir-fry a further 30 seconds. Pour in chicken stock and soy sauce. Bring to the boil, reduce heat and simmer, covered, 3 minutes.

6 Stir blended cornflour and water into sauce and cook until thickened.

SERVES 4

1 *Pull tentacles and intestines out of squid. Pull 'feather' out of squid and discard, as shown.*

2 *Rinse body and tentacles and peel skin from body. Drain well. Halve body lengthwise and score surface.*

Prawns Chow Mein

CRABMEAT SAUCE OVER BROCCOLI

1 tablespoon vegetable oil

1 slice fresh ginger root

1 clove garlic, crushed

750 g broccoli florets

¼ teaspoon salt

1 teaspoon light soy sauce

½ teaspoon sugar

2 tablespoons dry sherry

3 tablespoons fish stock or water

250 g crabmeat, fresh, frozen or canned

1 tablespoon shredded red capsicum (pepper), blanched

SAUCE

1 tablespoon dry sherry or white wine

¼ teaspoon salt

pinch pepper

1 cup (250 ml) fish stock

1 tablespoon cornflour blended with 2 tablespoons stock or water

1 Heat oil in a wok. Add ginger and garlic and cook until golden; remove. Add broccoli, stirring to coat with oil. Stir in salt, soy sauce, sugar, sherry and stock. Cook covered for 3 to 4 minutes until broccoli is bright green. Avoid overcooking.

2 Remove to serving platter and keep warm.

3 TO MAKE SAUCE: Heat sherry, salt, pepper and stock. Stir in blended cornflour and stock to thicken. When boiling, stir in crabmeat. Simmer 2 to 3 minutes. Pour sauce over broccoli, garnish with capsicum (pepper) and serve.

SERVES 4 TO 6

PRAWNS CHOW MEIN

10 Chinese mushrooms, soaked in warm water 20 minutes

2 tablespoons oil

2 stalks celery, sliced

125 g bamboo shoots, sliced

250 g bean sprouts, washed

250 g water chestnuts, drained and sliced

½ cup (125 ml) chicken stock

1 tablespoon dry sherry

1 tablespoon soy sauce

500 g school prawns, shelled

❖ **HINT**

Blend a large quantity of cornflour with water in a jar. Store in refrigerator and shake jar to mix before using.

1 Drain mushrooms, squeeze dry and discard stalks. Slice caps into strips. Heat oil in a wok. Add celery, bamboo shoots, mushrooms, bean sprouts and water chestnuts. Stir-fry about 2 minutes until vegetables are tender but crisp.

2 Pour in stock and sherry. Increase to high and bring to the boil. Reduce heat and stir in soy sauce and prawns. Cover and cook for 3 minutes. Remove from heat and serve immediately.

SERVES 4

BUTTERFLY PRAWNS

4 tablespoons plain flour

¼ teaspoon salt

1 egg, beaten

4 tablespoons beer or water

12 green (uncooked) king prawns

12 bacon strips cut 1 cm x 5 cm

24 small broccoli florets, blanched

2 tablespoons seasoned cornflour

1½ cups (375 ml) vegetable oil, for deep- frying

lemon wedges, to serve

1 Sieve flour and salt. Stir in egg and beer to form batter. Cut prawns through centre lengthways to the tail.

2 Shell and devein prawns, retaining tail. Wrap one strip of bacon around tail end of each prawn. Insert toothpicks to fasten. Place one broccoli floret onto each side of toothpick. Wrap each half of prawn around broccoli and fasten onto toothpick. Sprinkle prawns with cornflour. Lightly coat with batter. Do not batter the tail.

3 Heat oil. Fry prawns one at a time until tail turns pink, 2 to 3 minutes. Drain well. Serve with lemon and dip sauce of your own choice.

SERVES 2

Butterfly Prawns

WHOLE FISH IN BLACK BEAN SAUCE

750 g whole fish, cleaned and scaled (fish cutlets or fillets can also be used)

½ teaspoon salt

1 tablespoon plain flour

½ cup (125 ml) vegetable oil

½ teaspoon chopped fresh ginger root

½ teaspoon chopped garlic

1 tablespoon black beans, chopped

2 teaspoons dry sherry

2 teaspoons soy sauce

½ teaspoon sugar

1 cup (250 ml) fish stock or water

2 teaspoons cornflour blended with 1 tablespoon water

2 medium spring onions, chopped

1 tablespoon shredded red capsicum (pepper), blanched 1 minute in boiling water

1 Score fish on both sides. Season lightly with salt, then coat with flour.

2 Heat oil in a pan. Add fish and fry on both sides until golden. Remove to serving plate and keep hot. Pour off excess oil from pan leaving 1 tablespoon. Reheat, add ginger, garlic and beans, stir-fry 1 minute. Stir in sherry, soy sauce, sugar and stock. When boiling, stir in blended cornflour and water to thicken.

3 Add spring onions. Spoon over fish and garnish with capsicum (pepper).

SERVES 6

STIR-FRIED CRAB, GINGER AND SPRING ONIONS

2 large live crabs

2 tablespoons oil

1 clove garlic, crushed

3 thin slices fresh ginger root, finely chopped

1 bunch spring onions, sliced

¾ cup chicken stock (180 ml)

1 tablespoon soy sauce

1 tablespoon sherry

¼ teaspoon sugar

dash sesame oil

2 teaspoons cornflour blended with 2 tablespoons water

1 Cut green crabs in half and segment them. Heat oil in a wok. Add garlic, ginger and spring onions, and stir-fry for 30 seconds. Add crab pieces and stir-fry to coat with oil. Pour in stock, soy sauce, sherry, sugar and sesame oil and bring to the boil.

2 Cook covered until crab shells turn pink. Stir in blended cornflour, bring to the boil and serve.

SERVES 4

❖ **HINT**

Chinese cooking requires more preparation time than cooking time. Many dishes can actually be cooked in less than 10 minutes. To reduce the preparation time, many convenient ingredients are now available from Chinese foodstores and supermarkets. Rice, which is available in conventional white or brown, long- or short-grain, can now be replaced by the quick-cooking variety in both white and brown, saving 50 per cent of the cooking time.

SIMMERED WHOLE FISH

1 kg whole fish

1½ litres water

2 spring onions, cut in large pieces

2 thin slices fresh green ginger root, finely chopped

2 tablespoons sherry

1 tablespoon soy sauce

4 tablespoons oil

4 spring onions, sliced finely

2 slices red ginger, finely sliced

2 tablespoons soy sauce

1 teaspoon sesame oil

1 Scale fish, leaving head and tail intact. Score, rinse under cold water and drain.

2 Bring water to the boil. Add spring onions, ginger, sherry, soy sauce and 2 tablespoons oil to the water, and return to boil.

3 Place fish on a skimmer and lower into the boiling liquid. Reduce heat, cover and simmer gently 5 minutes. Turn off heat completely and leave, covered, for 20 to 25 minutes. Remove the fish carefully onto a serving platter. Sprinkle over finely sliced spring onions, red ginger and soy sauce. Heat remaining 2 tablespoons oil with sesame oil until sizzling, and pour over fish.

SERVES 4

Whole Fish in Black Bean Sauce

CRAB FOO YUNG

4 eggs

1 teaspoon soy sauce

½ teaspoon chilli sauce

2 teaspoons sherry

250 g fresh or canned crabmeat

3 tablespoons oil

6 Chinese mushrooms, soaked in warm water 20 minutes

6 spring onions, finely diced

SAUCE

1 cup (250 ml) chicken stock

2 teaspoons soy sauce

1 tablespoon cornflour blended with 1 tablespoon water

1 Beat eggs lightly in a bowl. Stir in soy and chilli sauces with sherry. Shred crabmeat.

2 Heat 1 tablespoon oil in a wok. Discard mushroom stalks and slice caps. Stir-fry mushrooms and spring onions for 2 minutes; add crabmeat and stir-fry 1 minute.

3 Remove wok from heat. Remove the mixture to a bowl, cool a few minutes and combine with egg mixture.

4 Heat 2 tablespoons oil in wok. Add a quarter of mixture and cook until the omelette is just set and lightly browned on the underside. Turn and cook for 1 minute. Place omelette on a serving plate. Repeat to make a total of 4 omelettes.

5 TO MAKE SAUCE: bring stock, soy sauce and blended cornflour and water to the boil, stirring constantly. Simmer 1 minute.

SERVES 2

FISH BALLS

1 kg firm white, unfrozen fish fillets

2 eggs

1 tablespoon ginger wine

2 teaspoons cornflour

½ teaspoon salt

pinch white pepper

stock or water

Crab Foo Yung

1 Cut fish into 2 cm cubes. Blend in a food processor with remaining ingredients. Shape mixture into 2 cm balls, with wet hands. Add balls to boiling stock or water to cover. Cook over medium heat 4 minutes, drain. Once cooked, fish balls will keep refrigerated for several days. Use in soups, add to stir-fried seafood combinations or deep-fry and serve with various sauces.

MAKES APPROXIMATELY 20

BRAISED ABALONE WITH CHINESE CABBAGE

1 tablespoon vegetable oil

1 teaspoon fresh chopped ginger root

½ teaspoon chopped garlic

500 g choy sum cabbage, cut into 5 cm lengths

1 teaspoon sugar

2 teaspoons dry sherry

½ cup (125 ml) reserved canned abalone liquid

1 teaspoon sesame oil

1 tablespoon oyster sauce

1 tablespoon soy sauce

2 teaspoons cornflour

600 g canned abalone, drained and thinly sliced (retain liquid)

3 tablespoons water

1 Heat oil. Add ginger, garlic and cabbage stems. Stir-fry 1 minute. Add cabbage leaf, sugar, sherry and abalone liquid. Cook until vegetable is bright green. Arrange cabbage on serving platter and keep warm.

2 Add sesame oil, oyster and soy sauces to pan. Blend cornflour with remaining liquid. Stir in to thicken when boiling. Reduce heat, and fold in abalone slices, to heat through briefly. Extended cooking will toughen abalone. Arrange slices over cabbage. Spoon over sauce and serve at once.

SERVES 6 TO 8

Braised Abalone with Chinese Cabbage

HONEYED PRAWNS

2 tablespoons oil

1 clove garlic, crushed

1 slice fresh ginger root, finely chopped

750 g green (uncooked) prawns, shelled with tail intact

¼ cup (80 g) honey

2 teaspoons soy sauce

sesame seeds

1 Heat oil in a wok. Add garlic and ginger and stir-fry for 30 seconds. Add prawns in two batches and stir-fry until pink. Remove the first batch before cooking the second. Pour over combined honey and soy sauce, toss quickly.

2 Serve sprinkled with sesame seeds.

SERVES 4

MEAT

Chinese cooking uses rice and noodles as the basic
staples of each meal, fleshed out with vegetables and garnished
with meat. Western tastes have traditionally been more accustomed
to larger quantities of meat, but Chinese recipes are now appreciated for
providing an inexpensive, nutritious and healthy balance of
ingredients with an amazing variety of flavours provided
by exotic but easily obtainable spices and herbs.

Beef, lamb and pork are the main kinds of meat used
and often form the centrepiece of a special celebratory occasion. The
techniques include steaming, simmering, braising, toasting and stir-frying.

Spicy Beef Satay and Cantonese Beef (page 40)

SLICED BEEF WITH OYSTER SAUCE

1½ tablespoons vegetable oil

½ teaspoon chopped garlic

500 g grilling steak, thinly sliced

1 teaspoon soy sauce

1 tablespoon dry sherry

¾ cup (180 ml) beef stock

1 tablespoon cornflour

2 tablespoons oyster sauce

1 teaspoon soy sauce

1 teaspoon sugar

½ teaspoon salt

1 Heat oil in a pan. Add garlic and stir briefly. Add a third of beef. Stir-fry 1 minute until it changes colour. Remove and repeat with remaining slices.

2 Return beef to pan. Add soy sauce and sherry, and cook for 1 minute. Pour in ½ cup (125 ml) stock.

3 Blend cornflour with oyster sauce, remaining stock, soy sauce, sugar and salt. Stir in to thicken. Serve at once.

SERVES 6

❖ **HINT**

To slice steak, cut into three or four portions. Place in freezer until firm. Cut thinly into diagonal slices.

SPICY BEEF SATAY

500 g grilling steak, cut in thin strips

1 tablespoon soy sauce

1 teaspoon sesame oil

2 teaspoons curry paste

3 tablespoons sesame paste

2 tablespoons dry sherry

2 tablespoons vegetable oil

1 Combine steak with soy sauce and sesame oil. Marinate 15 minutes.

2 Thread three to four slices on each satay stick. Leave 2 cm at the pointed end of stick without meat. A thin strip of foil can be wound around the blunt end of each stick to decorate.

❖ **HINT**

Soak bamboo satay sticks in water so they won't burn.

3 Combine curry paste, sesame paste and sherry. Spread thinly over beef. Brush with oil and cook under a preheated grill 1 to 2 minutes on each side.

SERVES 4

CANTONESE BEEF

4 tablespoons vegetable oil

2 medium onions, peeled and finely shredded

4 large tomatoes, skinned, cut in eighths

1 teaspoon sugar

½ teaspoon salt

1 tablespoon black beans, chopped

1 teaspoon chopped fresh ginger root

1 teaspoon chopped garlic

500 g grilling steak, cut in thin strips

2 tablespoons soy sauce

1 cup (250 ml) beef stock

1 tablespoon cornflour blended with 2 tablespoons stock or water

green tops of spring onions, sliced

1 Heat 2 tablespoons oil. Add onions, stir-fry 2 minutes. Add tomatoes, sugar and salt; stir-fry 1 minute. Cover and cook until tomatoes are just tender and retain shape. Remove to a bowl.

2 Heat remaining oil, add black beans, ginger and garlic. Stir-fry 1 minute. Add beef and cook over high heat until colour changes, 2 to 3 minutes. Add soy sauce, tomato mixture and beef stock.

3 Stir in blended cornflour and stock to thicken, without breaking tomato pieces. Serve garnished with spring onion tops.

SERVES 6

STEP-BY-STEP TECHNIQUES

STEAMED BEEF BALLS WITH WATER CHESTNUTS

1 cup (200 g) uncooked rice

500 g topside steak, minced

3 spring onions, finely chopped

1 teaspoon finely chopped fresh ginger root

2 water chestnuts, finely chopped

1 egg, lightly beaten

1 tablespoon soy sauce

2 teaspoons sherry

green vegetable leaves

soy sauce and chilli sauce, to serve

1 Place rice in a bowl, cover with water and soak for 1 to 1½ hours. Drain well and spread out on a tray to dry.

2 Combine steak, spring onions, ginger, water chestnuts, egg, soy sauce and sherry; mix until well blended. Form mixture into balls about 4 cm in diameter.

3 Roll each ball in rice until completely covered. Place balls on green vegetables in a steamer basket, leaving enough space between so they don't touch each other.

4 Place in a steamer and steam for 30 minutes over gently boiling water. Serve with soy and chilli sauces for dipping.

SERVES 4

1 *Prepare fresh ingredients by chopping finely. Form mixture into balls and roll in rice to coat.*

2 *Place balls on green leafy vegetables in a steamer basket, leaving space between balls so they don't touch.*

Steamed Beef Balls with Water Chestnuts

For best results, buy topside steak and mince it yourself. There are two methods of mincing.

Trim the meat and cut into largish pieces. Use one or two cleavers, one in each hand, and keep chopping until the meat is minced. Place a damp kitchen cloth under the board to deaden the noise.

Trim the meat and mince in a processor or use a mincer.

BEEF WITH SNOW PEAS (MANGETOUT)

500 g snow peas (mangetout)

3 tablespoons oil

2 teaspoons oyster sauce

500 g rump steak

2 cloves garlic, peeled and finely chopped

2 thin slices fresh ginger root, shredded

1 tablespoon soy sauce

1 red chilli, seeded and sliced

1 Top and tail snow peas (mangetout) and wipe with a damp cloth if necessary. Heat 1 tablespoon oil in a wok, add snow peas (mangetout) and stir-fry for 1 minute. Add oyster sauce and toss to coat. Remove and keep warm.

2 Trim meat and cut into four pieces. Heat remaining oil, add meat, garlic and ginger and cook until meat is sealed on both sides. Remove and cut meat into strips. Return to the wok and continue stir-frying for a further 5 minutes. Sprinkle with soy sauce. Serve topped with sliced chilli.

NOTE: If snow peas (mangetout) are not in season, Chinese broccoli or spinach may be substituted.

SERVES 4

GINGERED BEEF

1 teaspoon grated fresh ginger root

⅓ cup (80 ml) soy sauce

2 teaspoons cornflour

500 g rump steak, trimmed and thinly sliced across the grain

4 Chinese mushrooms, soaked in warm water 20 minutes

¼ cup (80 ml) oil

5 cm piece fresh ginger root, shredded

125 g canned bamboo shoots, drained and diced

1 In a large bowl combine grated ginger, soy sauce and cornflour.

2 Add meat and mix well. Allow to marinate for 1 hour, stirring occasionally. Drain mushrooms, remove stems and discard. Slice mushroom caps.

3 Remove meat from marinade and reserve. Heat oil in a wok over moderate heat. Add ginger and stir-fry for 3 minutes. Add meat, bamboo shoots and mushrooms and stir-fry until meat is cooked. Add marinade and heat through. Serve with rice or boiled noodles.

SERVES 4

CELLOPHANE BEEF

Each diner breaks open the envelopes with chopsticks and eats the contents from the paper.

170 g beef fillet

18 x 15 cm squares cellophane paper

1 tablespoon sesame oil

18 thin rings of carrot, parboiled

6 snow peas (mangetout), stems removed, cut into thirds

1 medium onion, peeled and finely chopped

oil, for deep-frying

shredded lettuce, to serve

MARINADE

½ teaspoon chopped garlic

3 tablespoons soy sauce

1 tablespoon dry sherry

½ teaspoon sugar

¼ teaspoon pepper

1 tablespoon vegetable oil

1 Chill beef and cut into 18 thin slices.

2 Combine garlic, soy sauce, sherry, sugar, pepper and oil. Add beef and stir to coat. Marinate 1 hour. Discard marinade.

3 Arrange cellophane sheets in diamond shape. Brush each sheet lightly with sesame oil. Place one slice of carrot, snow pea and ½ teaspoon onion in centre of lower half of paper. Top with one slice of beef. Fold up lower corner to cover beef. Fold left and right corners to centre. Fold lower section up

once more to centre line. Fold top corner down like an envelope and tuck in securely. Repeat until all the packages are made.

4 Heat oil to 150°C (300°F). Deep-fry a few envelopes at a time for 5 minutes. Drain well and arrange three envelopes each on six plates of shredded lettuce.

SERVES 6

FILLET STEAK CHINESE-STYLE

375 g piece fillet steak

1 tablespoon soy sauce

1 tablespoon hoisin sauce

1 tablespoon dry sherry

pinch five spice powder

2 tablespoons oil

¼ teaspoon salt

1 large onion, peeled and cut into eighths

½ teaspoon chopped fresh ginger root

1 teaspoon chopped garlic

1 level tablespoon cornflour

3 tablespoons beef stock

½ teaspoon sesame oil

spring onion greens, to serve

1 Freeze beef briefly until firm, then cut into thin slices.

2 Combine beef, soy and hoisin sauces, sherry and five spice, and marinate for 15 minutes. Remove beef and set marinade aside.

3 Heat 1 tablespoon oil in a pan. Add salt and onion and stir-fry 1 minute. Remove onion with a slotted spoon and set aside. Reheat remaining tablespoon of oil in pan and add ginger, garlic and beef. Stir-fry 1 to 2 minutes, until beef just loses its pinkness. Do not overcook or it will become tough. Return onion to pan.

4 Blend cornflour and stock and stir in to thicken. Sprinkle over sesame oil and serve garnished with green tops of spring onions.

SERVES 6

Fillet Steak Chinese-style

DEEP-FRIED SZECHUAN PORK

1 kg pork ribs, cut in 2½ cm dice

2 teaspoons chopped fresh ginger root

4 tablespoons brown sugar

3 tablespoons soy sauce

2 tablespoons dry sherry

½ teaspoon five spice powder

1½ cups (375 ml) vegetable oil

SZECHUAN SAUCE

2 tablespoons vegetable oil

3 red chillies, chopped

2 teaspoons chopped ginger root

2 teaspoons chopped garlic

½ medium onion, peeled and chopped

2 tablespoons dry sherry

4 tablespoons sugar

4 tablespoons tomato sauce

4 tablespoons white vinegar

1 Place ribs in a saucepan, cover with cold water and bring to the boil. Simmer 30 minutes; drain well.

2 Combine ginger, sugar, soy sauce, sherry and five spice powder. Add ribs, stirring to coat. Marinate 3 hours; drain and discard marinade.

3 Heat oil. Deep-fry ribs in small amounts until golden and tender. Drain well.

4 TO MAKE SAUCE: Heat oil in a pan. Add chillies, ginger, garlic and onion. Fry until tender. Add sherry, sugar, tomato sauce and vinegar. Simmer 10 to 15 minutes.

5 Add ribs, stirring to coat well. Simmer 10 minutes and serve hot.

SERVES 6

Pork Balls with Ginger and Deep-fried Szechuan Pork

PORK BALLS WITH GINGER

8 dried Chinese mushrooms, soaked in warm water 20 minutes

750 g minced lean pork

2½ cm piece fresh ginger root, finely chopped

4 canned water chestnuts, finely chopped

1 egg

1 tablespoon soy sauce

4 tablespoons cornflour

½ cup (125 ml) oil

1 bamboo shoot, diced

1 red capsicum (pepper), diced

1 green capsicum (pepper), diced

SAUCE

½ cup (125 ml) vinegar

½ cup (125 ml) sherry

2 tablespoons sugar

2 tablespoons tomato sauce

¼ to ½ teaspoon chilli sauce

1 tablespoon soy sauce

3 teaspoons cornflour blended with 2 tablespoons water

1 Drain mushrooms, discard stems and slice caps finely.

2 Combine minced pork with ginger, water chestnuts, egg, soy sauce and half the cornflour. Shape into small balls and roll in remaining cornflour.

3 Heat ⅓ cup (80 ml) oil in a wok. Fry pork balls in batches until crisp and brown. Test one to see if it is cooked. Remove and drain on kitchen paper.

4 Combine all sauce ingredients except cornflour paste.

5 Heat 2 tablespoons oil in the wok and stir-fry all the vegetables for 3 minutes. Pour over sauce and cook for a further 3 minutes. Thicken with blended cornflour. Pour vegetables and sauce over pork balls.

SERVES 4

Braised Pork Fillet in Peking Sauce

BRAISED PORK FILLET IN PEKING SAUCE

400 g pork fillets, thinly sliced

1 teaspoon cornflour

1 tablespoon soy sauce

1 tablespoon dry sherry

1 tablespoon stock

**350 g Chinese spinach, blanched
in boiling stock for 1 minute**

2 tablespoons vegetable oil

2 tablespoons hoisin sauce

½ teaspoon sesame oil or seeds

1 Combine pork with cornflour, soy sauce, sherry and stock. Let stand 15 minutes. Puree spinach, arrange on a serving platter and keep warm.

2 Heat oil in a wok. Stir-fry pork for 2 to 3 minutes. Remove from oil.

3 Reheat oil, add hoisin sauce. When hot, return pork. Stir-fry to reheat and coat with sauce. Add sesame oil. Serve over spinach.

SERVES 4 TO 6

SWEET AND SOUR PORK

500 g lean pork, cut in 2 cm dice

½ teaspoon salt

1 tablespoon flour

1 teaspoon dry sherry

1 egg yolk

6 tablespoons cornflour

1 tablespoon vegetable oil

1 teaspoon chopped fresh ginger root

1 teaspoon chopped garlic

½ red capsicum (pepper), cut in 2 cm dice

½ green capsicum (pepper), cut in 2 cm dice

180 g Chinese mixed pickles, sliced

½ cup (125 ml) water

1 tablespoon cornflour

3 tablespoons sugar

3 tablespoons white vinegar

3 tablespoons tomato sauce

¼ cup (60 ml) pickle juice

1½ cups oil (375 ml), for deep-frying

1 Combine pork, salt, flour, sherry and egg yolk in a bowl. Let stand 15 minutes. Roll pork in cornflour just before deep-frying.

2 Heat oil in a saucepan. Add ginger and garlic, and stir-fry 30 seconds. Add capsicums (peppers) and pickles. Blend water, cornflour, sugar, vinegar, tomato sauce and pickle juice. Stir into vegetables until mixture thickens. Keep warm.

3 Heat deep-frying oil. Cook pork in four batches for 5 minutes each. Remove and drain.

4 Reheat oil, refry pork 3 to 5 minutes. Drain well. Arrange on a serving platter. Spoon over sauce and serve at once.

SERVES 6

BRAISED NORTHERN LAMB

500 g boneless lamb

3 tablespoons soy sauce

3 tablespoons dry sherry

1 tablespoon sugar

1 teaspoon five spice powder

2 tablespoons vegetable oil

1 teaspoon chopped garlic

1 teaspoon chopped fresh ginger root

1 medium onion, cut in 2 cm cubes

1 teaspoon Szechuan peppercorns, ground

2 cups (500 ml) stock

3 potatoes, peeled and cut in 2½ cm dice

1 Combine lamb, soy sauce, sherry, sugar and five spice powder. Marinate 1 hour. Turn lamb pieces occasionally. Drain lamb, reserving marinade.

2 Heat oil in a pan. Add lamb and fry until golden and sealed on all sides.

3 Add garlic, ginger, onion and peppercorns. Stir-fry 2 minutes. Add reserved marinade and stock to cover. Bring to the boil. Simmer covered 1½ hours.

4 Add diced potatoes, and continue cooking 30 minutes or until tender.

SERVES 6

CHAR SUI

750 g boneless pork

1 tablespoon honey combined with 1 tablespoon hot water

MARINADE

2 tablespoons soy sauce

1½ tablespoons dry sherry

3 tablespoons hoisin sauce

1 teaspoon five spice powder

1 teaspoon sesame paste

1 teaspoon brown sugar

1 slice fresh ginger root

1 clove garlic, crushed

2 tablespoons vegetable oil

dash red food colouring

1 **TO MAKE MARINADE:** Combine marinade ingredients in bowl.

2 Cut pork into strips 3 cm x 15 cm. Pierce with a skewer. Add to marinade, stirring to coat. Let stand 1 hour or overnight in refrigerator.

3 Roast pork Chinese style on a rack over a pan of water, at 200°C (400°F) for 15 minutes. Baste with marinade. Reduce heat to 175°C (340°F). Roast a further 10 minutes.

4 Brush pork with honey mixture on each side, and continue cooking for 10 minutes.

5 Slice pork thinly. Serve hot or cold or in combination recipes.

SERVES 4 TO 6

❖ **MARINATING**

Marinate foods overnight for tenderness and flavour.

POULTRY

Duck and chicken are favourite fare in China and the
Chinese have created many interesting ways of preparing poultry. Drying,
smoking and curing are methods used with duck as well as roasting,
simmering, steaming and, of course, stir-frying. Many of the
same methods are used for chicken.

Whole chickens from Chinese specialty shops often come
complete with head and feet. The reason for this is that the beak and feet
give an indication as to the age of a chicken – they should be pliable.
Simply cut the neck and feet off and use in the stock pot.

If using a frozen chicken, make sure it is completely
defrosted before cooking. Do not defrost the chicken in the
refrigerator - this will take up to 24 hours.

When purchasing a fresh duck, make sure the oil sacs in the
tail have been removed before cooking. Ducks are sometimes trussed
and immersed in boiling water to remove the excess oil that duck,
as a water bird, has under its skin. Always pierce the skin
of a whole duck several times before cooking.

*Five Spice Chicken and
Shanghai-style Chicken (page 50)*

SHANGHAI-STYLE CHICKEN

1 medium onion, peeled and chopped

1 carrot, peeled and chopped

1 stalk celery, chopped

6 fresh parsley stalks

1 slice fresh ginger root

1 teaspoon white peppercorns

2 bay leaves

6 cups (1½ litres) cold water

1½ kg chicken

2 bunches fresh green asparagus

2 tablespoons toasted sesame seeds, to sprinkle

SAUCE

2 tablespoons vegetable oil

1 onion, peeled and finely sliced

½ teaspoon chopped garlic

2 red chillies, seeded and chopped

1 tablespoon oyster sauce

1 tablespoon soy sauce

1 cup (250 ml) chicken stock

salt and pepper

1 tablespoon cornflour

1 Cook chicken by placing vegetables, seasonings and water into a large saucepan. Bring to the boil, add chicken and simmer until tender. Remove chicken meat from carcass in strips. Set aside.

2 Cut 1 to 2 cm from root end of each asparagus stalk if tough. Scrape stems lightly with a peeler or small sharp knife. Wash well.

3 Re-tie asparagus in bunches. Cook in boiling salted water 6-8 minutes. Refresh in cold water.

4 TO MAKE SAUCE: Heat oil in a saucepan. Sauté onion and garlic 2 to 3 minutes and add chillies. Blend oyster sauce, soy sauce, stock, salt, pepper and cornflour together. Add to onion mixture and stir until boiling.

5 Arrange cooked asparagus on a serving platter. Top with chicken strips. Spoon sauce over chicken and sprinkle with sesame seeds. Serve hot.

QUICK VARIATION: Use canned asparagus spears. Cook chicken in a microwave on HIGH (100%) for 27 minutes. Prepare sauce while chicken is cooking.

SERVES 6 TO 8

FIVE SPICE CHICKEN

1½ kg chicken

4 spring onions, shredded

MARINADE

1 teaspoon chopped garlic

3 tablespoons soy sauce

2 tablespoons vegetable oil

½ teaspoon five spice powder

½ teaspoon sugar

1 Combine marinade ingredients. Brush mixture inside and over chicken. Let stand 30 minutes on a rack over a pan of water.

2 Drain chicken and roast Chinese style at 180°C (350°F) until tender. Baste and turn chicken four times during cooking for even browning.

3 Chop chicken Chinese style. Serve hot garnished with spring onions.

QUICK VARIATION: Place drained chicken in a glass dish on a microwave roasting rack. Cook uncovered 27 minutes on HIGH (100%), turning and basting every 10 minutes.

SERVES 6 TO 8

❖ **HINT**

When cooking, add longest cooking ingredients to pan or wok first.

STEP-BY-STEP TECHNIQUES

1 *Remove leg and thigh by cutting lengthways between thigh and breast.*

2 *Halve chicken by cutting along the backbone from the parson's nose to the neck.*

3 *Remove wings and separate drumsticks from thighs at the joint.*

4 *Divide wings into two pieces at the joints, and chop drumsticks and thighs into three pieces each. Slice breasts into three or four pieces depending on the size of the chicken.*

CRISP SPICED CHICKEN

1½ kg chicken

1 teaspoon five spice powder

1 tablespoon cornflour

oil, for deep-frying

lemon wedges and spring onions, to serve

1 Wash and clean chicken. Dry thoroughly and chop through the bone into 10 or 12 pieces. Combine five spice powder and cornflour and toss with chicken.

2 Heat oil in a wok and deep-fry chicken pieces in batches, for 5 minutes; drain well. Reheat the oil and deep-fry chicken until golden brown and cooked. Drain on absorbent kitchen paper.

3 Serve hot with rice, lemon wedges and spring onions.

NOTE: If you find five spice powder very pungent, reduce the quantity to ½ teaspoon the first time you make the dish.

SERVES 4

HONEY LEMON CHICKEN

1 kg fresh chicken pieces

2 tablespoons soy sauce

1 tablespoon dry sherry

juice 2 lemons, strained

2 to 3 tablespoons honey

2 tablespoons vegetable oil

1 teaspoon chopped fresh ginger root

1 teaspoon chopped garlic

¼ teaspoon salt

1½ cups (375 ml) chicken stock or water

**1 tablespoon cornflour blended with
2 tablespoons cold water**

slices of fresh lemon, to serve

*Smoked Chicken and
Braised Chicken with
Peking Sauce*

1 Pierce chicken pieces with a skewer. Combine soy sauce, sherry, lemon juice and honey. Brush over chicken pieces and let stand 30 minutes.

2 Heat oil. Add ginger, garlic and salt. Add drained chicken pieces and brown evenly. Pour off excess oil, add marinade and stock. Simmer covered 45 minutes until tender. Turn chicken pieces twice during cooking. Remove chicken and place on a serving platter. Stir blended cornflour and water into sauce. When boiling, strain and spoon over chicken pieces. Serve with lemon.

SERVES 6

BRAISED CHICKEN WITH PEKING SAUCE

500 g boned chicken breast, sliced

½ teaspoon salt

1 egg white, beaten

1½ cups (375 ml) vegetable oil

1 clove garlic, crushed

1 slice fresh ginger root

1 tablespoon vegetable oil

2 onions, cut in eighths

1 red capsicum (pepper), cut in 2 cm dice

2 tablespoons hoisin sauce

1 tablespoon dry sherry

60 g vermicelli noodles

1 Mix chicken slices with salt and egg white. Heat oil. Add garlic and ginger, remove when brown. Fry chicken pieces until white. Drain well on kitchen paper.

2 Heat 1 tablespoon oil. Add onions and capsicum (pepper), stir-fry 2 minutes. Stir in hoisin sauce, sherry and chicken to reheat.

3 Cut noodles into 5 cm lengths. Fry in hot oil until they puff up. Drain well on kitchen paper. Arrange on a serving platter and top with onion mixture.

SERVES 6

SMOKED CHICKEN

1½ kg chicken

2 tablespoons brown peppercorns

1 tablespoon salt

2 litres water

4 spring onions

3 slices fresh ginger root

2 whole star anise

1 cinnamon stick

1 cup (250 ml) soy sauce

½ cup (125 g) sugar

½ cup (60 g) plain flour

½ cup (60 g) dry tea leaves

1 tablespoon sesame oil

1 Clean and wipe chicken. Fry peppercorns and salt for 1 minute in a wok. Rub into chicken and allow to stand for 2 hours.

2 Bring water to the boil in a large pan. Add spring onions, ginger, star anise, cinnamon and soy sauce and simmer 10 minutes. Add chicken and cook for 10 minutes over low heat, turning once. Remove chicken and allow to cool.

3 Put sugar, flour and tea leaves in a wok, and cover with a rack. Sit chicken on its side on rack. Cover tightly and smoke for 45 minutes to 1 hour, over a low heat, turning chicken halfway through. Remove chicken from wok and brush with sesame oil; cool.

4 Chop Chinese style and arrange on a platter.

SERVES 6

SWEET AND SOUR SESAME CHICKEN

1½ kg chicken, jointed

3 tablespoons plum sauce

1 tablespoon vinegar

2 cups (500 ml) chicken stock

⅓ cup (80 ml) dry sherry

1 tablespoon finely chopped fresh ginger root

1 onion, quartered

160 g canned straw mushrooms

2 stalks celery, sliced

220 g canned water chestnuts

220 g canned bamboo shoots, drained and sliced

2 tablespoons cornflour blended with water

1 tablespoon sesame seeds

1 Preheat oven to 180°C (350°F). Arrange chicken in an ovenproof dish. Combine plum sauce, vinegar, stock, sherry and ginger and pour over chicken. Cover and bake 40 minutes.

2 Add vegetables, return to oven and cook a further 15 minutes. Remove chicken and vegetables to a heated serving dish.

3 Thicken remaining liquid with blended cornflour and water. Bring to the boil and simmer 2 minutes. Pour over chicken. Sprinkle with sesame seeds and serve hot with rice.

SERVES 6

❖ **HINT**

Toast sesame seeds in a dry pan and store in a jar. Keep a stock of oven-roasted nuts to use as a garnish.

PEKING DOILIES

1¼ cups (310 ml) water

2 cups (250 g) plain flour, sifted

oil or sesame oil, or a combination of the two

1 In a pan, bring water to the boil. Add flour, all at once, and stir very quickly with a wooden spoon to combine. Remove from pan and knead mixture on a floured board until smooth, about 10 minutes. Cover with a damp towel and stand for 10 minutes.

2 Form the dough into a long roll 3 cm in diameter. Cut into 1 cm thick slices. Flatten to a 6 mm thickness and brush one side of half the rounds with a little oil. Place one unoiled round on top of the oiled side of another. Dust each pair with flour and roll out to a very thin pancake, about 10 to 12 cm in diameter. Roll from the centre, turning the pancake a little after each roll to ensure a perfect circle of even thickness.

3 Heat an ungreased wok or griddle over low to medium heat. Bake one pancake at a time for about 1 minute on each side or until lightly coloured.

4 Transfer to a platter, separate the two halves and keep covered with a towel until all pancakes are ready. Peking doilies can be made in advance, kept in the refrigerator and reheated by steaming for 8 to 10 minutes.

**MAKES 15 TO 25 DOILIES
(DEPENDING ON THICKNESS)**

PEKING DUCK

2 kg duck

½ to ¾ cup (125 to 180 ml) water

4 tablespoons honey

Peking doilies

spring onion curls

½ cucumber

½ to ¾ cup (125 to 180 ml) hoisin sauce or plum sauce

1 Choose a fresh duck with neck and skin intact. Wash duck, immerse in boiling water, lift out and dry thoroughly inside and out. Hang duck overnight in a cool airy place, to allow the skin to dry thoroughly.

2 Dissolve honey in water and brush skin until completely saturated with honey. Hang duck to dry completely for about 6 hours or until the skin is dry and slightly hardened by the honey.

3 Meanwhile, prepare Peking doilies and spring onion curls. Peel cucumber and cut in half lengthways. Scoop out the seedy centre part and cut into strips.

4 To separate the skin from the flesh of the duck, insert a straw immediately underneath the skin and blow through it. Place duck on a rack over a drip pan. Roast in a 180°C (350°F) oven without basting for 1½ to 2 hours or until skin is browned and crisp.

5 With a very sharp knife, slice off skin and cut into squares. Carve meat in thick slices and serve separately during the meal. Take a doily and top with one or two pieces of skin, spring onion curls, cucumber strips and hoisin sauce. Roll doily to eat.

SERVES 6

EIGHT JEWEL DUCK

2 kg boned duck

salt

1 cup (200 g) uncooked rice

1 tablespoon vegetable oil

½ teaspoon chopped fresh ginger root

½ teaspoon chopped garlic

125 g pork, minced

4 Chinese mushrooms, soaked in warm water 20 minutes

60 g bamboo shoots

6 water chestnuts

4 uncooked or 10 dried prawns, soaked and diced

2 thin slices ham, diced

¼ cup (40 g) toasted almonds, chopped

1 tablespoon soy sauce

1 tablespoon dry sherry

1 spring onion

❖ **PEKING DUCK**
Sometimes only the skin is eaten and the meat used as an ingredient for other dishes.

1 Lightly salt duck inside and out. Cut all vegetables into small dice. Cook rice using Chinese Rice recipe.

2 Heat a wok. Add oil, ginger, garlic and pork. Stir-fry 4 minutes. Add mushrooms, bamboo shoots, chestnuts, prawns, ham and almonds. Stir-fry until hot. Add soy sauce, sherry and spring onion. Fold in rice. Allow mixture to cool.

3 Secure neck opening with a poultry skewer. Pack mixture into cavity of duck. Fasten with poultry skewer. Reshape duck and brush lightly with oil. Place a sheet of foil on top of a cake rack over a baking dish containing 3 cm cold water.

4 Arrange duck, breast side up on foil. Roast at 200°C (400°F) for 30 minutes. Reduce heat to 175°C (340°F) and cook 1 to 1½ hours until duck is golden and tender. Turn duck occasionally for even browning.

5 Remove skewers and carve. Serve hot or cold.

SERVES 8

Peking Duck served with Peking Doilies

*Roast Duck
and Plum Sauce*

❖ **Hint**

*To plump ducks, place
fresh ducks in boiling
water to cover. Allow to
stand 5 minutes. This
firms the duck flesh before
roasting or steaming.
Drain well, then follow
recipe instructions.*

ROAST DUCK
AND
PLUM SAUCE

2 to 2½ kg duck

1 tablespoon vegetable oil

3 tablespoons plum sauce

MARINADE

3 tablespoons chicken stock

1 tablespoon brown sugar

2 tablespoons soy sauce

1½ tablespoons honey

1 teaspoon five spice powder

1 Combine marinade ingredients in a large basin. Add duck and baste with mixture. Marinate 1 hour. Baste and turn duck every 15 minutes.

2 Drain duck, reserving marinade. Roast duck Chinese style on a rack over a pan of water at 180°C (345°F) for 2 hours, basting with marinade every 30 minutes.

3 Chop duck into serving pieces and arrange on a serving platter. Heat oil in a saucepan, add plum sauce and heat through. Pour over duck.

SERVES 6 TO 8

STIR-FRIED DUCK AND BITTER MELON

1 tablespoon fermented black beans

1 clove garlic

2 kg duck

1 tablespoon hoisin sauce

1 tablespoon sherry

½ teaspoon chilli sauce

1 tablespoon cornflour

250 g fresh or canned bitter melon

4 tablespoons oil

1 cup (250 ml) chicken stock

extra 2 teaspoons cornflour

2 tablespoons water

1 Soak black beans in water for 10 minutes. Drain and mash beans with garlic. Cut duck meat from breast and legs and reserve carcass for making stock. Cut meat across the grain into 1 cm thick slices.

2 Mix hoisin sauce, sherry, chilli sauce and cornflour. Add duck slices and mix well. Marinate for 20 minutes. If using fresh bitter melon, wash and drain. Remove stalks, halve bitter melon lengthways and remove seedy centre. Cut into thin slices. Bring plenty of salted water to boil, add bitter melon and parboil 4 minutes.

3 Rinse under cold running water until completely cooled; drain. If using canned bitter melon, drain liquid, rinse under cold running water, drain and slice.

4 Heat half the oil in a wok. Add black bean mixture and stir-fry for 30 seconds. Add duck slices and stir-fry until lightly coloured. Remove and keep warm. Add remaining oil, heat and stir-fry the bitter melon for 1 to 1½ minutes. Add stock and bring to the boil. Return duck slices to wok, reduce heat, cover and simmer until heated through. Blend cornflour with water and add to wok; cook until sauce is thickened.

SERVES 4 TO 6

DEEP-FRIED DUCK IN LYCHEE SAUCE

1½ to 2 kg fresh duck

2 eggs

¾ cup (180 g) plain flour

2 tablespoons ginger wine

½ teaspoon salt

1½ cups (375 ml) vegetable oil, for deep frying

LYCHEE SAUCE

1 tablespoon vegetable oil

½ teaspoon chopped garlic

½ red capsicum (pepper), cut in 2 cm dice

½ green capsicum (pepper), cut in 2 cm dice

200 g lychee fruit

½ cup (125 ml) lychee juice

¼ cup (60 ml) water

½ cup (125 ml) white vinegar

⅓ cup (80 g) sugar

1 tablespoon tomato sauce

1 tablespoon cornflour blended with 2 tablespoons water

1 Cut duck meat into 2½ cm pieces, leaving skin intact. Beat eggs, blend in flour, wine and salt to form a batter. Add duck pieces and stir to coat.

2 Heat oil, add duck in batter six at a time. Cook until golden. Drain well and keep warm on a serving platter. To make sauce, heat oil in a wok. Add garlic, capsicums and lychees, and stir-fry 1 minute. Remove from pan.

3 Stir in lychee juice, water, vinegar, sugar and tomato sauce. Bring to the boil. Stir in blended cornflour and water. When boiling, return vegetables and lychee fruit to reheat. Spoon over duck cubes.

SERVES 6

❖ **TOASTING RAW NUTS**

Add nuts to boiling water to cover. Cook 3 to 5 minutes. This softens nuts to the centre. Drain and dry.

Heat enough oil to cover nuts. Add nuts and toast them until they turn a pale ivory colour, stirring during cooking. Drain well and cool before using. Nuts will be crisp and cooked to the centre.

HEALTHY
VEGETARIAN FARE

One of the most remarkable aspects of Chinese cooking is the approach to vegetables. They are of the utmost importance. This emphasis is due partly to the influence of the Buddhist monks, who established strict vegetarian rules. Small wonder this resulted in the development of extraordinary skill in preparing vegetables.

The main difference between the Chinese method of cooking vegetables and the Western way is that in the Chinese way, vegetables are cooked only long enough to bring out all their qualities of crispness, tenderness and brightness of colour. The vegetables are served at the peak of their flavour. This does not mean that they are served raw; even in salads, the vegetables will usually be cooked briefly.

Cutting is of the utmost importance in the preparation of vegetables. Vegetables are cut, blanched and parboiled in such a way that even the final cooking can be completed at one time, even though the textures of the individual vegetables differ greatly. The soft leafy vegetables require less cooking than the tougher ones.

Noodle Soup with Quail Eggs, Stir-fried Bean Curd
with Szechuan Sauce and Bean Sprout Salad (page 60)

NOODLE SOUP WITH QUAIL EGGS

4 to 6 cups (1 to 2½ litres) water

250 g fresh egg noodles

¾ teaspoon salt

2 teaspoons soy sauce

1 teaspoon peanut oil

few drops sesame oil

pinch white pepper

12 quail eggs, boiled and shelled

3 spring onions, finely cut

2 litres boiling vegetable stock

1 Bring water to the booil. Add salt and noodles. Cook 3 to 5 minutes until just tender. Drain, then rinse in cold water. Drain again.

2 Place noodles in a large tureen. Add soy sauce, peanut and sesame oils and pepper. Toss well to mix.

3 Arrange eggs and spring onions over noodles. Pour over stock and serve at once with the sauce of your choice. Quail eggs taste particularly delicious with Szechuan Sauce.

SERVES 6

SZECHUAN SAUCE

2 tablespoons vegetable oil

3 red chillies, chopped

2 teaspoons chopped ginger root

2 teaspoons chopped garlic

½ medium onion, chopped

2 tablespoons dry sherry

4 tablespoons sugar

4 tablespoons tomato sauce

4 tablespoons white vinegar

1 Heat oil in a pan. Add chillies, ginger, garlic and onion. Fry until tender.

2 Add sherry, sugar, tomato sauce and vinegar, and simmer 10 to 15 minutes.

MAKES APPROXIMATELY 1 CUP (250 ML)

STIR-FRIED BEAN CURD WITH SZECHUAN SAUCE

3 tablespoons vegetable oil

¼ teaspoon salt

2 spring onions, cut in 2 cm lengths

500 g firm bean curd, cut in 2 cm dice

4 tablespoons Szechuan Sauce

1 Heat oil in a wok. Add salt, white of spring onions and bean curd cubes. Stir-fry gently to heat through.

2 Add Szechuan Sauce and simmer 3 minutes. Stir in spring onion greens and serve.

SERVES 6 TO 8

BEAN SPROUT SALAD

500 g soy bean sprouts

2 tablespoons light soy sauce

1 tablespoon white vinegar

1 teaspoon sugar

½ teaspoon sesame oil

250 g snow pea (mangetout) sprouts

1 bean curd cake, cut in julienne strips

¼ red capsicum (pepper), cut in julienne strips

1 Blanch soy bean sprouts in boiling water for 1 minute. Refresh in cold water and drain well.

2 Combine soy sauce, vinegar, sugar and sesame oil in a bowl, add soy bean and snow pea (mangetout) sprouts. Toss to coat with dressing. Cover and chill 20 minutes.

3 Arrange salad on a platter. Garnish with bean curd and capsicum (pepper).

NOTE: Snow pea (mangetout) sprouts are available from most Chinese food stores and some groceries.

SERVES 8

STEP-BY-STEP TECHNIQUES

1 *Cut bean curd cakes in half. Make a pocket in each half to contain filling.*

2 *Carefully stuff cakes with filling.*

3 *Place cakes on a shallow heatproof dish and steam for about 25 minutes.*

STUFFED BEAN CURD

6 cakes bean curd

1½ tablespoons oil

1 thin slice fresh ginger root, finely chopped

1 clove garlic, crushed

2 stalks celery, or 6 leaves cabbage or other seasonal green vegetable, cut into 4 cm diamonds

¾ cup (180 ml) stock

2 tablespoons soy sauce

1 tablespoon sherry

1 tablespoon cornflour blended with 2 tablespoons water

FILLING

250 g tempeh, grated

6 spring onions, minced

2 water chestnuts, minced

½ tablespoon soy sauce

1 tablespoon sherry

1 egg yolk

1 Cut bean curd cakes in half. Make a pocket in each half to contain filling, taking care not to break bean curd. In a bowl, combine filling ingredients. Stuff bean curd carefully with this mixture. Place bean curd in a shallow heatproof dish and steam for about 25 minutes.

2 About 5 minutes before the steaming is completed, heat oil in a wok. Add ginger and garlic. Stir-fry 1 minute until golden brown. Discard ginger and garlic. Increase heat, add celery and stir-fry for 1 minute. Add chicken stock, soy sauce and sherry.

3 Reduce heat, cover and continue cooking for 1½ minutes. Stir blended cornflour and water into vegetables. Cook 30 seconds until thickened. Remove dish with bean curd from the steamer. Serve with rice.

SERVES 4

Braised Vegetables

2 Heat oil in a wok. Add garlic and ginger, and stir for 1 minute. Add vegetables and stir-fry over high heat about 2 minutes. Add vinegar, sugar, sherry and chicken stock and bring to the boil. Stir in blended cornflour and water to thicken.

SERVES 4

ASPARAGUS IN THE SNOW

500 g fresh green asparagus, tough ends removed

1 slice fresh ginger root

1 tablespoon dry sherry

2 tablespoons vegetable stock

2 egg whites

1 tablespoon cornflour

1 cup (250 ml) seasoned vegetable stock

1 Place asparagus, ginger, sherry and stock into pan. Cook over high heat 3 to 4 minutes until crispy tender. Place asparagus on a serving platter, reserving cooking liquid.

2 To make sauce, beat egg whites with asparagus cooking liquid. Blend cornflour with seasoned stock. Heat until thickened. Whisk 2 tablespoons heated thickened stock into egg mixture. Whisk egg mixture into remaining sauce. Serve hot.

SERVES 4

SWEET AND SOUR VEGETABLES

1 green capsicum (pepper)

1 medium onion

2 stalks celery

2 carrots

2 tablespoons oil

1 clove garlic, crushed

2 thin slices fresh ginger root, finely chopped

75 g shredded canned bamboo shoots

3 tablespoons vinegar

2 tablespoons sugar

1 tablespoon sherry

2 tablespoons stock

1 tablespoon cornflour blended with 2 tablespoons water

1 Remove membrane and seeds from capsicum (pepper) and cut into 5 cm long diamond shapes. Peel onion, halve lengthways and cut each half into 1 cm wide strips lengthways. Cut celery in 5 cm pieces diagonally. Cut carrots in a rolling cut, diagonally into 4 cm pieces. Parboil vegetables for 3 to 4 minutes.

BRAISED VEGETABLES

2 tablespoons oil

1 teaspoon sesame oil

1 clove garlic, crushed

1 teaspoon finely chopped fresh ginger root

500 g prepared mixed vegetables

½ cup (125 ml) hot water

1 tablespoon oyster sauce

1 tablespoon soy sauce

2 teaspoons cornflour blended with 1 tablespoon water

1 In a wok heat oil and add sesame oil, garlic and ginger. Add vegetables and stir-fry 2 minutes. Add hot water, oyster and soy sauces. Simmer 4 minutes.

2 Push vegetables to one side of wok, add blended cornflour and water and stir until sauce thickens. Fork vegetables through sauce and serve with boiled rice.

SERVES 4

STIR-FRIED BROCCOLI AND BEAN CURD IN OYSTER SAUCE

500 g broccoli

2 tablespoons oil

fresh ginger root, sliced

1 clove garlic, finely chopped

¼ cup canned bamboo shoots, shredded

2 cakes bean curd, cut in 1 cm cubes

2 tablespoons oyster sauce

1 tablespoon soy sauce

½ cup (125 ml) stock

1 teaspoon cornflour blended with 2 tablespoons water

1 Cut off florets from broccoli stems. Discard tough ends and cut wide stems in half lengthways. Cut in 2 cm pieces diagonally. Parboil in a large quantity of salted water 3 to 4 minutes. Drain and rinse broccoli under cold running water. Cool completely.

2 Heat oil in a wok until very hot. Add ginger and garlic. Stir-fry 1 minute until ginger is lightly browned. Discard ginger and garlic. Add drained broccoli and stir-fry 1 minute. Add bamboo shoots, bean curd, sauces and chicken stock. Bring to the boil, reduce heat, cover and simmer for 2 minutes. Stir in blended cornflour and water to thicken the sauce.

SERVES 4

STIR-FRIED BEAN SPROUTS

375 g bean sprouts

2 tablespoons oil

1 thin slice fresh ginger root, finely chopped

½ green capsicum (pepper), sliced

½ medium onion, cut in wedges

12 spring onions, sliced

2 thin slices ham, shredded

2 tablespoons stock combined with ½ tablespoon sherry

1 Pour boiling water over bean sprouts and let stand 20 seconds.

2 Refresh in cold running water, drain and dry. Heat oil in a wok. Add ginger and stir-fry 30 seconds. Add capsicum (pepper), onion and spring onions and stir-fry 1½ minutes. Add bean sprouts and ham and stir-fry 30 seconds. Add combined stock and sherry and bring to the boil. Remove from heat and serve.

SERVES 4

Stir-fried Broccoli and Bean Curd in Oyster Sauce

Mock Duck Foo Yung and Crunchy Omelette in a Nest

1 tablespoon light soy sauce

60 g vermicelli noodles, fried and lightly crushed

1 spring onion, shredded

1 Heat oil in a pan. Add onion and stir-fry with mock duck, peas and corn 2 minutes. Stir in eggs, salt, pepper and soy sauce. Draw edges of mixture into the centre until set, without allowing mixture to dry.

2 Place noodles on a serving platter. Place egg mixture on top, leaving a noodle border. Top with spring onion shreds.

SERVES 8

VEGETABLE CHOW MEIN

1½ cups (375 ml) vegetable oil

250 g fresh noodles

2 tablespoons vegetable oil

½ teaspoon chopped garlic

1 small onion, shredded

1 medium carrot, sliced and parboiled

160 g bamboo shoots, sliced

150 g mini corn

8 fresh mushrooms, thickly sliced

200 g fresh mustard cabbage, cut into 3 cm lengths

1 tablespoon soy sauce

½ cup (125 ml) vegetable stock

1 tablespoon cornflour blended with ¼ cup (60 ml) vegetable stock

1 Heat oil in a pan. Add one-third of the noodles. Fry until crisp, turning over with tongs during cooking. Drain well and repeat until noodles are cooked. Set aside on a warm serving platter.

2 Heat 2 tablespoons oil. Add garlic, onion, carrot, bamboo shoots and corn. Stir-fry 1 minute. Add mushrooms, cabbage, soy sauce and stock. Cook covered 2 minutes.

3 Stir in blended cornflour and stock to thicken. Serve hot over fried noodles.

SERVES 4 TO 6

MOCK DUCK FOO YUNG

2 tablespoons vegetable oil

1 medium onion, shredded

280 g canned vegetarian mock duck, thinly sliced

60 g green peas, blanched

60 g corn kernels, cooked

6 eggs, beaten

salt and pepper

STEAMED DIM SUM

24 wonton skins

lettuce leaf, for steaming

FILLING

250 g firm bean curd, finely chopped

125 g soy beans, cooked and mashed

1 spring onion, finely cut

1 tablespoon chopped fresh coriander leaves

2 tablespoons celery, finely chopped

2 Chinese mushrooms, soaked in warm water 20 minutes and chopped

2 teaspoons soy sauce

¼ teaspoon sesame oil

salt and pepper

1 Combine all filling ingredients. Place 2 teaspoons filling onto each wonton skin. Gather outer edges of skin around filling. Press gently so that filling rises to the top of skin. The base should be flat.

2 Place a lettuce leaf in steamer. Arrange dim sum on top, leaving space between each to prevent sticking.

3 Steam 10 minutes. Serve with soy vinegar dip.

MAKES 24 DIM SUM

CRUNCHY OMELETTE IN A NEST

2 tablespoons vegetable oil

1 medium onion, finely shredded

2 stalks celery, finely chopped

½ red capsicum (pepper), finely chopped

5 fresh mushrooms, thickly sliced

125 g bean sprouts, root removed

salt and pepper

6 eggs, beaten

1 spring onion, finely chopped

1 tablespoon chopped cashew nuts

1 large potato nest

1 Heat oil in a wok. Add onion, celery and capsicum (pepper), and stir-fry 2 minutes. Add mushrooms, bean sprouts and seasonings and stir-fry 1 minute. Pour in eggs. Fold into vegetables until mixture sets. Turn over and cook for 1 minute.

2 Remove and cut into strips. Place into potato nest. Sprinkle with spring onions and cashews, and serve at once.

SERVES 4 TO 6

BEAN CURD OMELETTE

2 tablespoons vegetable oil

¼ teaspoon salt

2 spring onions, finely chopped

60 g peas, blanched in boiling water 1 minute

125 g bean curd, cut in 1 cm dice

6 eggs, beaten

1 tablespoon light soy sauce

1 Heat oil in a wok. Add salt, spring onions, peas and bean curd. Stir-fry 1 minute.

2 Pour in eggs. Cook over medium heat until mixture begins to set. Draw outer edges to the centre until eggs form a scrambled egg consistency, moist and retaining shape.

3 Sprinkle with soy sauce before serving.

SERVES 4 TO 6

BARBECUED BEAN CURD

250 g firm bean curd

3 tablespoons char sui sauce

1 Pierce bean curd with toothpick. Coat evenly with char sui sauce and marinate 30 minutes.

2 The bean curd can be oven-roasted Chinese style for 20 minutes at 175°C (340°F) or pan-fried in 3 to 4 tablespoons oil, turning onto each side during cooking.

3 Cool and slice. Use for stir-fry combinations, soups or in fried rice.

MAKES 250 G

❖ **HINT**

Instant noodles are available both plain and flavoured with chicken, prawn, beef, curry or vegetables. They can be used in soups, or stir-fried with a topping. Their cooking time of 2 minutes has captured the noodle market. Dried noodles can be boiled then mixed with a small amount of oil and refrigerated in portion sizes several days before use.

STIR-FRIED HONEY DUCK

280 g can vegetarian mock duck

2 teaspoons vegetable oil

½ teaspoon chopped garlic

2 spring onions, sliced

1½ tablespoons light soy sauce

1½ tablespoons dry sherry

1 tablespoon honey

**1 teaspoon cornflour blended with
2 teaspoons stock**

1 Cut mock duck into even-sized 2 to 3 cm pieces.

2 Heat oil in a pan. Add garlic and spring onions and stir-fry 1 minute. Add soy sauce, sherry and honey, simmer 2 minutes. Add vegetarian duck pieces and simmer 15 minutes. Thicken with blended cornflour and stock and serve.

SERVES 4

❖ **MOCK DUCK**

First made in China in the tenth century AD, mock duck is made from wheat flour, gluten, safflower oil, soy bean extract, sugar, salt and water. Considered a delicacy, it is available canned, and can be used to replace real duck in most recipes.

BEAN CURD AND POTATO ROLLS

250 g boiled potato, mashed

250 g firm bean curd, mashed and drained

2 spring onions, finely chopped

salt and pepper

2 large spring roll skins

cold water or egg white

oil, for deep frying

1 Combine potato, bean curd, spring onions, and salt and pepper in a bowl. Halve mixture and shape each half into a roll, 10 cm long.

2 Arrange spring roll skins in a diamond shape. Brush edges with cold water or egg white. Place one roll on each skin. Fold lowest point of skin over filling and roll once. Fold left and right points into centre. Brush edges again. Roll up firmly to cook.

3 Fry in oil to cover until golden and crisp.

4 To cook using the oven method, place rolls onto baking tray and bake at 200°C (400°F) for 20 minutes until golden.

SERVES 4 TO 6

VEGETABLE SPRING ROLLS

2 tablespoons vegetable oil

6 medium Chinese mushrooms, soaked in warm water 20 minutes and sliced

2 medium onions, sliced

½ teaspoon chopped garlic

1 teaspoon chopped fresh ginger root

300 g Chinese cabbage, shredded

100 g celery, sliced

100 g beans, sliced

100 g carrot, grated

60 g soy bean sprouts

100 g water chestnuts

3 tablespoons light soy sauce

1 teaspoon sesame oil

pinch pepper

1 tablespoon cornflour blended with

2 tablespoons vegetable stock

12 large spring roll skins

1 egg white or 2 tablespoons water

100 g firm bean curd, sliced

4 tablespoons plum sauce

1 Heat oil in a wok. Fry mushrooms, onions, garlic and ginger 1 minute. Add remaining vegetables and stir-fry 2 minutes. Blend in soy sauce, sesame oil and pepper.

2 Stir in blended cornflour and vegetable stock to thicken pan juices. Place mixture on a tray to cool. Divide filling into twelve portions. Arrange spring roll skins in diamond shapes with pointed end towards you. Brush edges with egg white. Place a portion of filling onto each skin, top with sliced bean curd. Fold lower point over filling. Fold left and right points into centre. Brush with egg white again. Roll up firmly and stand on sealed edge.

3 Rolls can be deep fried two or three at a time in vegetable oil until golden, or oven-baked at 180°C (350°F) for 15 to 20 minutes. Serve with warm plum sauce.

SERVES 4 TO 6

TOSSED RICE NOODLES WITH CHOP SUEY

3 tablespoons vegetable oil

1 teaspoon chopped fresh ginger root

1 onion, shredded

100 g broccoli florets

½ cup (125 ml) vegetable stock

250 g fresh mushrooms, cut in 1 cm slices

200 g bean sprouts, root removed

160 g bamboo shoots, sliced

60 g water chestnuts, sliced

300 g bean curd cakes, diced

2 tablespoons dry sherry

1 teaspoon sesame oil

450 g rice noodles, sliced

GARNISH

1 egg omelette, cut into thin strips

1 spring onion, finely chopped

1 tablespoon almond slivers, toasted

1 Heat oil in a wok. Add ginger, onion and broccoli, and stir-fry 1 minute. Add stock and cook covered 2 minutes. Add mushrooms, bean sprouts, bamboo shoots, water chestnuts, bean curd, sherry and sesame oil. Fold in noodles. Cover and simmer 1 to 2 minutes to heat through. Serve hot.

2 Garnish with shredded egg, spring onion and almond slivers.

SERVES 4 TO 6

Tossed Rice Noodles with Chop Suey

LOW FAT
AND LOW CHOLESTEROL
DELIGHTS

The Chinese diet is traditionally low in fat and Chinese
fare can be readily adapted for low cholesterol cooking. In part
this is because meals are based on rice with delicious sauces made
from vegetables, fruits and spices plus a garnish of animal
protein in the form of meat, fish or chicken.

By making your own sauces at home using fresh,
natural ingredients, removing all visible fat from meat, chicken or
duck and by quickly stir-frying in a non-stick pan or wok using a little
stock or water, you can continue to enjoy many of your favourite recipes -
including spring rolls. Usually deep-fried, spring rolls can be
baked in the oven to produce a tasty appetiser
for a low cholesterol meal.

*Beef Fillet with Sweet and Sour Sauce
and Steamed Dim Sum (page 70)*

STEAMED DIM SUM

100 g eggless wonton skins

1 to 2 tablespoons peas

lettuce leaves, to steam

FILLING

250 g chicken, steamed and finely chopped

250 g firm white fish fillets, finely chopped

1 spring onion, finely cut

4 tablespoons chopped water chestnuts

4 Chinese mushrooms, soaked in warm water 20 minutes and finely chopped

1 tablespoon salt-reduced soy sauce

pinch pepper

DIP SAUCE

2 tablespoons salt-reduced soy sauce

1 tablespoon white vinegar

1 Mix all filling ingredients together. Place 2 to 3 teaspoons filling in the centre of each skin. Gather edges around filling and press so that filling comes up to the edge of each skin. Place a pea on top of filling. The dim sum should have a flat base and stand upright.

2 Place a few lettuce leaves into a bamboo steamer. Arrange dim sum on top with enough space between them so they don't touch. Steam covered 20 minutes. Serve with sauce.

3 TO MAKE DIP SAUCE: Combine ingredients in a small bowl.

SERVE 4 TO 6

BEEF FILLET WITH SWEET AND SOUR SAUCE

500 g fillet steak, cut in 1 cm dice

1 tablespoon salt-reduced soy sauce

¼ teaspoon five spice powder

SWEET AND SOUR SAUCE

1 cup (250 ml) unsweetened pineapple juice

1 tablespoon sugar

1 tablespoon white vinegar

1 tablespoon cornflour

1 tablespoon dry sherry

1 cup (250 ml) beef consomme

½ green capsicum (pepper), cut in 1 cm dice

¼ carrot, parboiled, cut in 1 cm dice

50 g unsweetened pineapple pieces

90 g diced Chinese mixed pickles

1 Combine diced steak with soy sauce and five spice powder and marinate 15 minutes. Heat a non-stick pan, add one-quarter of the steak and stir-fry 3 to 4 minutes. Remove from pan. Repeat with remaining beef. Set aside and keep warm.

2 Bring pineapple juice, sugar and vinegar to the boil. Blend cornflour, sherry and stock to a paste. Stir into pineapple juice to

thicken. Add vegetables, simmer 3 minutes. Add diced steak to heat through. Serve at once.

SERVES 4 TO 6

PUMPKIN AND FISH BALLS WITH BLACK BEAN SAUCE

500 to 750 g firm pumpkin or squash

350 g fish balls with parsley

1 cup (250 ml) vegetable stock

SAUCE

1 tablespoon black or yellow beans, chopped

1 level teaspoon chopped garlic

1 teaspoon chopped fresh ginger root

1½ tablespoons salt-reduced soy sauce

2 tablespoons dry sherry

½ teaspoon sugar

pinch pepper

1 tablespoon cornflour blended with 4 tablespoons vegetable stock

1 Remove seeds from pumpkin. Using a melon baller, prepare even-sized pumpkin balls. Heat stock, add pumpkin balls and cook until just tender. Drain, retaining stock.

2 Reheat stock in a non-stick pan, add beans, garlic, ginger, soy sauce, sherry, sugar and pepper. Simmer 2 minutes. Add fish balls. Simmer covered 4 to 5 minutes. Add pumpkin balls to reheat. Stir in blended cornflour and vegetable stock to thicken. Serve at once.

SERVES 4 TO 6

❖ **NOTE**

Fish balls can be bought ready-made in Asian foodstores or can be made at home.

Pumpkin and Fish Balls with Black Bean Sauce

BEEF WITH CHILLI BEAN SAUCE

250 g fillet steak, thinly sliced

1 tablespoon dry sherry

¼ cup (60 ml) beef consomme

1 teaspoon chopped garlic

1 tablespoon chilli bean sauce

1 large onion, cut into eighths

2 teaspoons cornflour

1 teaspoon salt-reduced soy sauce

3 tablespoons vegetable stock or water

1 Combine sliced steak and sherry. Heat a non-stick pan, add beef and stir-fry 2 minutes. Remove from pan and set aside.

2 Reheat pan, add consomme, garlic, chilli bean sauce and onion, and simmer covered 2 minutes.

3 Return steak to pan. Blend cornflour with soy sauce and stock. Stir in to thicken and serve at once.

SERVES 4

❖ **HINT**

Soak bamboo satay skewers in water to prevent burning.

CHICKEN AND VEGETABLE SATAY

250 g chicken breast, skin removed, cut in 2 cm dice

1 tablespoon salt-reduced soy sauce

1 medium onion, quartered

¼ red capsicum (pepper), cut into 2 cm dice

8 button mushrooms

4 long bamboo satay sticks, soaked in water to prevent burning

¼ cup orange juice (60 ml)

1 Combine chicken with soy sauce and let marinate 15 minutes. Thread chicken, onion, capsicum (pepper) and mushrooms onto satay sticks. Place on a sheet of foil and brush with orange juice.

2 Grill under medium heat until chicken is white. Baste with orange juice frequently to prevent drying out. Serve with brown rice.

SERVES 4

FISH COCKTAILS WITH HONEY ORANGE SAUCE

500 g firm white fish fillets, cut in 3 cm dice

2 tablespoons salt-reduced soy sauce

2 tablespoons honey

3 tablespoons fresh orange juice, strained

1 slice fresh ginger root, shredded

cornflour (optional)

1 Combine fish pieces, soy sauce, honey and orange juice. Marinate 15 minutes.

2 Place fish and marinade in a shallow heatproof dish. Sprinkle with ginger. Cover with a lid or foil. Steam over boiling water 12 minutes.

3 Drain off liquid and reheat in a saucepan. Reduce by half or thicken with cornflour. Serve over fish pieces.

SERVES 4

BEEF AND BROCCOLI

250 g fillet steak, thinly sliced

2 teaspoons salt-reduced soy sauce

4 tablespoons vegetable stock

500 g broccoli florets

½ teaspoon sugar

½ teaspoon chopped fresh ginger root

3 teaspoons cornflour blended with 2 tablespoons vegetable stock

1 Combine diced steak with soy sauce, and let marinate 15 minutes. Heat a non-stick pan. Add beef and stir-fry 1 minute. Remove from pan and set aside.

2 Add stock to pan and bring to the boil. Add broccoli, sugar and ginger, and cook covered over high heat 3 minutes.

3 Return beef to pan. Stir in blended cornflour and stock to thicken. Serve at once.

SERVES 4 TO 6

Beef with Chilli Bean Sauce and Chicken and Vegetable Satay

Spaghetti Squash with Peking Sauce

1 Combine scallops with hoisin sauce. Thread onto skewers with diced onion. Place on sheet of foil and brush with a mixture of orange juice and soy sauce.

2 Grill under medium heat 2 to 4 minutes, until scallops are white. Brush with orange juice and soy sauce during cooking. The remaining juice can be thickened and served as a sauce.

SERVES 4

SPAGHETTI SQUASH WITH PEKING SAUCE

500 to 750 g spaghetti squash in one piece

1½ cups (375 ml) vegetable stock

SAUCE

250 g lean veal, minced

2 teaspoons dry sherry

½ cup onion, finely chopped

1 tablespoon canned yellow bean sauce

2 tablespoons salt-reduced soy sauce

1 tablespoon hoisin sauce

1½ cups (375 ml) seasoned vegetable stock

1 tablespoon finely chopped fresh coriander

1 **TO PREPARE SQUASH:** Leave skin on and remove seeds with a spoon. Place stock in a saucepan. Stand squash cut side up in saucepan, cover, and bring liquid to the boil. Simmer 20 minutes until squash is tender.

2 Remove squash and scrape out flesh in long strands from skin. Place on a warm serving platter.

3 **TO MAKE SAUCE:** Combine veal with sherry and onion in a non-stick pan. Stir-fry until veal loses its pink colour. Add bean paste, soy and hoisin sauces with stock and simmer 20 minutes.

4 The sauce can be thickened slightly if desired. Serve poured over spaghetti squash and garnish with fresh coriander.

SERVES 4

SWEET AND SOUR CABBAGE

3 tablespoons unsweetened pineapple juice

1 teaspoon chopped fresh ginger root

1 medium onion, cut into eighths

2 red capsicums (peppers), shredded

500 g cabbage, shredded

2 tablespoons sugar or substitute

2 tablespoons white vinegar

1 tablespoon salt-reduced soy sauce

1 tablespoon cornflour

¼ cup (60 ml) stock

❖ **HINT**

Blend a large quantity of cornflour with water in a jar. Store in refrigerator and shake jar to mix before using.

1 Heat pineapple juice in a non-stick pan. Add ginger, onion and capsicums (peppers), and stir-fry 2 minutes. Add cabbage and cook covered 2 minutes. Stir in sugar, vinegar and soy sauce.

2 Blend cornflour with stock. Stir in to thicken. Serve at once.

SERVES 4

SCALLOP SATAY

500 g fresh scallops or thick white fish fillets

2 tablespoons hoisin sauce

1 large onion, cut in 2 cm dice

8 small satay sticks, soaked in cold water

½ cup (125 ml) orange juice

1 tablespoon salt-reduced soy sauce

HOT SOUR BEAN CURD SOUP

6 cups (1½ litres) vegetable stock

1 tablespoon cornflour

1 teaspoon grated fresh ginger root

1 tablespoon dry sherry

1 tablespoon salt-reduced soy sauce

1 tablespoon white vinegar

pinch cayenne pepper

250 g firm bean curd, cut into 1 cm cubes

1 egg white, lightly beaten

lettuce leaves, shredded

1 Blend stock with cornflour and bring to the boil. Add ginger, sherry, soy sauce, vinegar and pepper. Simmer 2 minutes.

2 Add bean curd to heat through for 2 minutes. Pour in egg white. When set, add lettuce, serve at once.

SERVES 4 TO 6

VEAL SPRING ROLLS

250 g lean veal steak, finely chopped

2 teaspoons salt-reduced soy sauce

1 teaspoon sugar

2 tablespoons vegetable stock

4 Chinese mushrooms, soaked in warm water 20 minutes and shredded

250 g soy bean sprouts, root removed

1 onion, finely chopped

250 g cabbage, finely shredded

1 tablespoon cornflour blended with 2 tablespoons vegetable stock

12 large eggless spring roll skins

DIP

4 tablespoons plum sauce combined with few drops chilli sauce

1 Combine veal, soy sauce and sugar and stand 15 minutes. Heat vegetable stock in a non-stick frying pan. Add veal and stir-fry lightly. Add mushrooms, bean sprouts, onion and cabbage and stir-fry for a few minutes.

2 Stir in blended cornflour and stock to thicken pan juices. Remove mixture. Allow to cool.

3 Divide mixture into 12 portions. Arrange spring roll skins in diamond shapes. Place a portion of filling in centre. Fold bottom point over filling. Fold sides to centre. Brush with cold water. Roll up firmly. Place on an ungreased tray and bake at 200°C (400°F) 20 to 30 minutes. Serve with dip sauce.

SERVES 6

BRAISED MIXED VEGETABLES

½ cup (125 ml) vegetable stock

1 teaspoon chopped fresh ginger root

½ teaspoon chopped garlic

½ teaspoon sugar

125 g broccoli florets

1 large onion, cut into eighths

125 g snake beans, cut into 2½ cm lengths

125 g bamboo shoots, sliced

125 g straw mushrooms

1 tablespoon salt-reduced soy sauce

1 tablespoon oyster sauce

1 tablespoon dry sherry

2 teaspoons cornflour

1 Bring stock to the boil in a pan. Add ginger, garlic, sugar, broccoli, onion and beans. Cover, and cook on high heat 3 to 4 minutes. Add bamboo shoots and straw mushrooms.

2 Blend soy and oyster sauces with sherry and cornflour. Stir into vegetable mixture to thicken slightly. Serve at once.

SERVES 4 TO 6

❖ **HINT**

Braise long-cooking dishes in advance. Divide into portion serves and freeze.

ABOUT CHOLESTEROL

It is now clear that reducing the amount of fat in our diet has significant health benefits for us all. Fat, whether saturated or unsaturated, is a concentrated source of kilojoules (calories). In addition, high fat diets have been linked to the development of other diseases including gallbladder disease and some cancers. Recent research shows that reducing food fat, particularly saturated fat, has a more direct influence on blood cholesterol than does food cholesterol. For most people it is better to cut down on saturated fats than to eliminate nutritious foods such as eggs, shellfish and liver which are high in cholesterol. The following table lists the foods containing fat. These foods contain a mixture of saturated, monounsaturated and polyunsaturated fats. The food is classified according to the predominant fat.

SATURATED FAT Butter, cream, dripping, lard, copha; coconut oil, palm oil; many cheeses, ice cream, chocolate; meat fat, poultry skin; full cream dairy products; many commercial foods including snack foods, pies, pastries, biscuits, fast foods, chips.

MONOSATURATED FAT Olive oil, olives; peanut oil, peanuts, peanut butter; most nuts; avocado; egg yolk; margarine (unless labelled polyunsaturated); lean meat, chicken, salmon, tuna.

POLYUNSATURATED FAT Most vegetable oils, including safflower, sunflower, maize or corn, cotton seed, soya bean, grape seed, walnut, sesame; margarine, reduced-fat spreads and oils labelled polyunsaturated; seeds, including sunflower, pumpkin, sesame; nuts: walnuts, brazil nuts, pine nuts; fish, shellfish.

LOW CHOLESTEROL COOKING MADE EASY

REDUCE FATS Reduce your intake of all fats. Only 30 per cent of your total kilojoule (calorie) intake should come from fats, with saturated fats contributing no more than 10 per cent and unsaturated fats (poly- and monounsaturated) contributing the remaining 20%.

REDUCE CHOLESTEROL Reduce your cholesterol intake from foods to under 300 milligrams a day. Limit cholesterol-rich foods such as brains, liver, kidney, egg yolks, prawns, fish roe and squid.

REDUCE SALT Reduce your salt intake. Do not sprinkle salt on food or in cooking, and switch to salt reduced or no-added-salt products.

INCREASE FIBRE Increase your fibre intake. Oats, oat bran, barley, barley bran, rice, rice bran, dried beans, lentils, fruit and vegetables.

COLD SUMMER NOODLES

500 g eggless, curry flavoured noodles

6 cups (1½ litres) vegetable stock

250 g chicken breast, steamed and shredded

250 g fresh bean sprouts, roots removed and blanched

1 telegraph cucumber, cut in half lengthways and shredded

1 teaspoon chopped garlic

3 tablespoons vinegar

3 tablespoons salt-reduced soy sauce

1 Cook noodles in boiling stock 4 minutes. Drain and cool, discarding stock.

2 Combine chicken, bean sprouts and cucumber. Add garlic, vinegar and soy sauce. Add to noodles, toss to blend. Serve chilled.

SERVES 4

EGGPLANT (AUBERGINE) WITH BEAN CURD AND BASIL

1 tablespoon vegetable oil

1 teaspoon chopped garlic

250 g firm bean curd, cut in 2 cm dice

1 medium eggplant (aubergine), peeled and cut in 2 cm dice

4 ripe tomatoes, peeled and quartered

½ teaspoon sugar

¼ teaspoon dried basil

½ teaspoon salt

¼ teaspoon pepper

½ cup (125 ml) vegetable stock

1 Heat oil in a wok. Lightly fry garlic and bean curd. Add eggplant (aubergine), tomatoes, sugar, basil, salt, pepper and stock. Bring to the boil, then simmer gently until eggplant (aubergine) is tender. The mixture may be thickened slightly with cornflour if preferred.

SERVES 6

STIR-FRIED CHICKEN WITH BEAN SPROUTS

¼ cup (60 ml) vegetable stock

125 g fresh chicken breast, skinned and shredded

500 g bean sprouts, root removed

2 teaspoons cornflour

2 teaspoons dry sherry

¼ teaspoon sugar

1 tablespoon salt-reduced soy sauce

1 Heat stock in a non-stick pan. Add chicken strips and stir-fry 3 minutes. Add bean sprouts. Cook covered 2 minutes. Blend cornflour, sherry, sugar and soy sauce. Stir in to thicken. Serve at once.

2 Serve with spring onion shreds.

SERVES 4

CHICKEN AND VEGETABLE SOUP

200 g chicken breast, bones and skin removed

2 Chinese mushrooms, soaked in warm water 20 minutes and sliced

2 teaspoons dry sherry

6 cups (1½ litres) vegetable stock

⅓ stalk celery, sliced

½ carrot, cut in thin strips

1 teaspoon cornflour blended with 2 teaspoons stock or water

1 tablespoon finely chopped fresh coriander or spring onions

1 Cut chicken meat into thin strips. Cover with boiling water. Let stand 2 minutes. Drain, then repeat process - this ensures the chicken is free of any hidden fat. Sprinkle mushrooms with sherry and let stand.

2 Bring stock to the boil, add chicken, mushrooms, celery and carrots. Simmer covered 5 minutes. Blend cornflour with stock, stir in to thicken soup. When boiling, sprinkle soup with coriander and serve.

SERVES 4 TO 6

❖ **HINT**

Freeze fresh noodles, wonton skins and spring roll skins in recipe size amounts.

RICE
AND NOODLES

Rice and noodles are staple fare in the Chinese diet. Rice is grown and eaten primarily in the southern part of China. But even apart from the basic necessity of eating rice, to the Chinese the taste is the perfect accompaniment to all other foods. When sampling all the myriad taste elements of a Chinese meal, a spoonful of rice taken with the other food as well as in between brings a neutral element into play so that every new morsel can unfold all its full flavour and character.

Long grain rice is suitable for most dishes. When properly cooked, rice absorbs a great deal of water and will be dry and fluffy. Rice is either boiled or steamed. It is very important to wash the rice well to remove the excess starch which otherwise would make the rice too sticky. After it has been boiled or steamed, cooked rice can be fried. It should be completely cooled before it is fried.

Noodles are the food of the north. They are made mainly from grains but sometimes also from seaweed or the starch of mung peas. They can be boiled, steamed, soft fried, deep fried and used in soups.

Fresh Egg Noodle Baskets and Three Jewelled Chicken in Noodle Baskets (page 80)

POTATO NESTS OR BASKETS

500 g grated potato

2 tablespoons cornflour

salt and pepper

oil, for frying

1 Combine potato, cornflour and seasoning. Dip basket moulds or wire strainers into hot oil. Place 3 to 4 tablespoons potato mixture into the larger basket. Arrange to cover surface of basket. Place smaller basket on top. Holding the handles of both baskets together, dip into hot oil to cover.

2 When the potato sets, the smaller mould can be removed. Continue cooking until crisp and golden.

3 Use for serving deep- or stir-fried food.

MAKES 1 BASKET

❖ **ROAST DUCK**

Roast duck should be available from specialty Chinese shops, or you may prepare your own. Marinate duck pieces in char sui marinade and cook as for char sui.

CONGEE ROAST DUCK

¾ cup (150 g) uncooked rice

6 cups (1½ litres) water

2 small dried scallops, 2 tablespoons dried prawns or 1½ teaspoons salt

1 small piece dried tangerine or orange peel

½ roast duck, cut into bite-sized pieces

1 tablespoon sherry

2 tablespoons sliced spring onions

1 Place rice and water in a pan. Add scallops and tangerine peel. Bring to the boil over high heat. Reduce heat, cover and simmer for 45 minutes.

2 Add roast duck and sherry. Cover and simmer for at least 1 hour, stirring occasionally and adding some water if the congee becomes too thick. Remove tangerine peel and dried scallops, if desired. Top with spring onions and serve.

SERVES 4

THREE JEWELLED CHICKEN IN NOODLE BASKETS

vermicelli noodle baskets

FILLING

200 g boneless chicken breast, thinly sliced

1 teaspoon cornflour

2 teaspoons egg white

2 tablespoons vegetable oil

1½ tablespoons ginger in syrup, sliced

100 g canned lychees

100 g canned loquats

SAUCE

1 tablespoon cornflour

2 tablespoons light soy sauce

2 tablespoons white vinegar

2 tablespoons sugar

6 tablespoons lychee juice

1 Combine chicken, cornflour and egg white in a bowl. Heat oil in a wok. Stir-fry chicken until white. Add ginger, lychees and loquats.

2 Blend sauce ingredients. Heat in a pan, stir to form sauce and thicken.

3 Serve mixture evenly in noodle baskets.

MAKES 6 INDIVIDUAL BASKETS OR 2 LARGE BASKETS

❖ **VARIATIONS**

Fresh egg noodle baskets: Divide 60g of fresh egg noodles into 6 portions, and line 6 basket moulds. Cook as for Potato Nests.

Vermicelli nests or baskets: Cut 30 g of vermicelli noodles into 2½ cm lengths. Line a large mould and cook as for Potato Nests.

STEP-BY-STEP TECHNIQUES

CRISPY NOODLES

350 g egg noodles (preferably fresh)

2 tablespoons oil

1 onion, shredded

½ bunch celery, shredded

250 g chicken or pork, shredded

1 tablespoon soy sauce

oil, for deep-frying

1 Cook noodles. Drain, rinse well and set aside. After about 10 minutes, turn out noodles onto a tray and separate them with chopsticks or a fork.

2 Heat oil in a wok and stir-fry vegetables and meat together for about 5 to 6 minutes. While still crisp, season with soy sauce and keep warm.

3 Put noodles into a strainer, heat the oil for deep-frying and plunge strainer into the oil; fry until noodles are crisp then drain on absorbent kitchen paper. Turn onto serving dish and add meat and vegetable sauce.

SERVES 4

1 *Cook noodles, drain and rinse well. After 10 minutes, turn onto a tray and separate with chopsticks.*

2 *Heat oil in a wok and stir-fry meat and vegetables together for 5 to 6 minutes.*

3 *Put noodles in a strainer, heat oil for deep-frying and plunge strainer into the oil. Fry until crisp then drain on kitchen paper.*

FRIED RICE WITH BEEF AND ALMONDS

250 g lean steak, thinly sliced and shredded

1 tablespoon soy sauce

1 tablespoon cornflour

3 tablespoons vegetable oil

1 large onion, cut in fine shreds

1 medium capsicum (pepper), cut in fine shreds

½ teaspoon salt

2 cups (500 g) hot steamed rice

125 g almonds, toasted

GARNISH

spring onion shreds

extra toasted almonds

1 Combine steak, soy sauce and cornflour. Heat oil in a wok and add steak mixture. Stir-fry 2 minutes. Add onion, capsicum (pepper) and salt. Stir-fry 1 minute. Add rice and almonds, stir-frying to blend ingredients. This can be done off the heat

2 Place mixture into an oiled ring mould. Press down firmly. Turn out onto round serving plate, garnish and serve.

SERVES 6

❖ **HINT**

Deep-fry chow mein noodles, drain well and store in an air-tight container.

PORK FRIED RICE

1½ cups (300 g) uncooked rice

3 tablespoons oil

2 eggs, lightly beaten

1 clove garlic, bruised

1 slice fresh ginger root, roughly chopped

6 spring onions, cut in 1 cm pieces

250 g Chinese barbecued pork (char sui)

3 tablespoons soy sauce

1 Cook rice. Heat 1 tablespoon oil in a wok. Pour in beaten eggs to form a flat omelette; cook for 2 minutes. When bottom is set, flip over and cook for further 2 minutes. Remove from heat, roll up Swiss-roll style and cut into thin strips.

2 Heat remaining oil in wok, add garlic and ginger and cook until browned, drain and discard. Add spring onions and rice. Stir-fry 2 to 3 minutes. Add char sui and soy sauce, and stir-fry 1 minute. Add a little water if too dry. Spoon rice into a serving dish and garnish with egg strips.

SERVES 4

COMBINATION SEAFOOD CHOW MEIN

250 g crisp fried fresh egg noodles

125 g prawn meat, deveined

125 g scallops

125 g prepared squid

125 g sliced fish fillets

½ teaspoon chopped fresh ginger root

2 tablespoons cornflour

2 tablespoons light soy sauce

2 tablespoons sherry

4 tablespoons oil

½ teaspoon salt

4 stalks Chinese cabbage, cut in 2½ cm pieces

1 cup (150 g) sliced bamboo shoots

180 g straw mushrooms, sliced lengthways

1 Arrange crisp fried fresh egg noodles on serving platter and keep warm.

2 Combine seafood, ginger, cornflour, soy sauce and sherry, toss to coat.

3 Heat 2 tablespoons oil. Add seafood and stir-fry 2 to 3 minutes. Remove from pan.

4 Heat remaining oil. Add salt and Chinese cabbage stalks, and stir-fry 1 minute.

5 Add cabbage leaves, bamboo shoots and mushrooms. Cover and cook 2 minutes.

6 Return seafood to reheat. Serve over crisp noodles.

SERVES 6 TO 8

BARBECUED PORK CHOW MEIN

2 tablespoons vegetable oil

1 teaspoon chopped fresh ginger root

1 teaspoon chopped garlic

250 g Chinese barbecued pork (char sui)

4 Chinese mushrooms, soaked in warm water 20 minutes and sliced

60 g carrot, sliced and parboiled

200 g broccoli florets, blanched

60 g bamboo shoot, sliced

125 g bean sprouts, root removed

½ cup (125 ml) stock

2 tablespoons light soy sauce

1 tablespoon dry sherry

1 teaspoon sugar

1 tablespoon cornflour blended with 2 tablespoons water

250 g soft fried noodles

1 Heat oil in a wok. Add ginger, garlic, pork and stir-fry 1 to 2 minutes. Add vegetables, stock, soy sauce, sherry and sugar. Simmer covered for 2 minutes.
2 Stir in blended cornflour and water to thicken. Serve over hot noodles.

SERVES 6

Pork Fried Rice

❖ **FRIED RICE**

When cooking rice for fried rice, steam in advance. Spread onto a tray and refrigerate until required. Cooked rice will freeze and defrost well.

RICE

❖ **STEAMED RICE**
Rinse rice with cold water several times. Place rice in a medium-sized saucepan and cover with cold water to 2 cm above the rice. Bring to the boil. Stir once and cook uncovered until air bubble holes form. Reduce heat to low. Cover and steam for 20 minutes. Remove from heat and allow to stand covered 5 minutes. Stir rice grains with a fork to loosen, avoiding cutting through grains. Steamed rice will remain hot in the saucepan for over 30 minutes. During this time several stir-fry dishes can be prepared.

Rice is one of the best sources of nutrition and nourishment around the world. Brown rice is better value than white rice, but both can be useful in our diets, as they are:
❖ high in protein and dietary fibre
❖ high in vitamins and minerals – calcium, iron, thiamine, riboflavin and niacin
❖ low in fat, salt and sugar
❖ cholesterol-free
On the question of how much to use, the general rule is ½ cup (100 g) uncooked rice per person. If steaming, allow 2 cups (500 ml) water for the first cup of rice, and 1½ cups (375 ml) water for each additional cup of rice.

CHINESE RICE

2½ cups (500 g) uncooked rice

water

1 Wash rice in cold water until water runs clear. Place rice in saucepan and cover with water to 2½ cm above rice level. Bring to the boil, reduce heat to medium and continue cooking, uncovered, until water evaporates (air bubble holes will form through rice).
2 When water has evaporated, place lid on saucepan and continue cooking for 7 minutes on low heat. Do not stir or lift lid during last 7 minutes of cooking. If not using immediately, leave in covered pan.

SERVES 4 TO 6

FRIED RICE

2 cups (500 g) cold cooked rice

3 eggs, beaten lightly

2 tablespoons vegetable oil

90 g cooked prawn meat, cut in 5 mm dice (optional)

2 rashers cooked bacon, drained, cut in 5 mm dice or 125 g char sui

2 spring onions, cut in 5 mm dice

1 tablespoon light soy sauce

¼ teaspoon sesame oil

salt and pepper

1 Fold beaten eggs through rice.
2 Heat wok. Add oil by pouring it around the rim. This seals the wok and heats the oil quickly. Add rice and stir-fry over high heat; after a few minutes the grains will separate. Add prawns and bacon. Stir-fry 1 minute. Add remaining ingredients and stir-fry to blend flavours. Serve rice in a warm Chinese bowl to retain heat during serving.

SERVES 6

Fried Rice: Use chopsticks to separate grains of rice.

Add rice grains and stir-fry.

Pour in egg mixture.

NOODLES

In China, noodles are traditionally the food of the north. They are made mainly from grains, but sometimes also from seaweed or the starch of mung peas. Noodles are almost always made in thin threads, but there is considerable variety in texture, thickness and width. They can be boiled, steamed, soft-fried, deep-fried and used in soups. These days, they are often available from larger supermarkets and delicatessens, as well as from Asian foodstores and Chinese grocers.

DRIED NOODLES

Dried long-life egg and eggless noodles are available in various packs. The noodles can be thin, round or flat and come in 50 g bundles, usually 6 to 8 bundles per packet. Dried noodles are also available flavoured e.g. chicken, shrimp, beef and curry.

CHINESE NOODLES

1 to 1¼ litres water

1 teaspoon salt

250 g dried noodles

vegetable or sesame oil

TO SOFT-FRY NOODLES

4 tablespoons vegetable oil

½ teaspoon salt

1 Bring water to the boil. Add salt, then noodles. Stir with chopsticks to loosen each bundle. Cooking should be completed in 3 to 5 minutes. Do not overcook; remember noodles will also be fried. Drain well, rinse in cold water. Drain and spread loosely on a tray. Sprinkle with a little oil and refrigerate for 2 hours before frying.

2 Heat oil with salt. When very hot, carefully add cooked noodles. Use tongs or chopsticks to loosen noodles. Reduce heat and fry noodles for 2 minutes. Turn noodles over and cook another 2 minutes. The noodles should be lightly brown and crisp on the outside.

SERVES 4

FRIED NOODLES WITH CHICKEN AND VEGETABLES

250 g fresh egg noodles

oil, for deep-frying

1 whole chicken breast, skinned and boned

250 g green (uncooked) prawns, shelled

1 clove garlic, crushed

1 piece bamboo shoot, shredded

6 Chinese mushrooms, soaked in warm water for 20 minutes and sliced

125 g vegetables (e.g. celery, spring onions, beans), cut into matchsticks

½ cup (125 ml) stock

½ teaspoon cornflour

1 tablespoon soy sauce

pinch five spice powder

1 Divide noodles into four portions. Deep-fry each portion in hot oil until golden brown. Drain on absorbent kitchen paper.

2 Cut chicken meat into strips. Heat wok, add 1 tablespoon vegetable oil and stir-fry chicken and prawns with garlic. Add bamboo shoot, mushrooms and vegetables and stir-fry for a further 5 minutes.

3 Pour in stock, cornflour, soy sauce and five spice powder and simmer for 5 minutes.

4 TO SERVE: Place noodles on a plate and spoon over chicken and vegetables.

SERVES 4

Fried Noodles with Chicken and Vegetables

❖ **CRISP-FRIED FRESH EGG NOODLES**

Heat 1½ cups (375 ml) oil in a wok. Test temperature with a strand of noodle. If it crisps up quickly, the oil is the correct temperature. Separate 250 g fresh egg noodles into two batches. Carefully lower into the oil, one batch at a time. Cook 2 minutes, turn over with tongs and continue cooking until crisp and golden.

SAUCES AND DIPS

The Chinese have two main categories of sauces. A number of sauces are incorporated into the dish and have already been mixed with the other ingredients by the cook. The other group of sauces are served on the table as dipping sauces.

Marinades are also widely used in Chinese cooking to flavour and tenderise the food before it is actually cooked.

❖ PEPPER AND SALT MIX

Heat a wok until very hot. Add 3 tablespoons salt and 2 tablespoons Szechuan peppercorns or crushed peppercorns. Reduce the heat and stir 5 to 6 minutes or until salt is light brown. Crush peppercorns in a mortar and pestle and sift through a sieve. Store in a tightly covered jar.

SHERRY-SOY DIP

2 tablespoons sherry

2 tablespoons soy sauce

¼ teaspoon sugar

1 Combine all ingredients and stir together until the sugar has dissolved.

MAKES ¹/₃ CUP (80 ML)

SWEET AND SOUR GINGER SAUCE

½ cup (125 g) sugar

6 cm slice fresh ginger root, finely chopped

½ cup (125 ml) vinegar

½ cup (125 ml) pineapple juice

1 tablespoon sherry

1½ tablespoons cornflour blended with ⅓ cup (80 ml) water

125 g Chinese pickle, finely sliced

1 In a saucepan, combine sugar, ginger, vinegar, pineapple juice and sherry. Bring to the boil and stir in blended cornflour and water to thicken. Stir in Chinese pickle.

MAKES ABOUT 2 CUPS (500 ML)

PLUM SAUCE

10 fresh plums, pitted and finely chopped

¼ cup (35 g) dried apricots, soaked in warm water 1 hour and finely chopped

1 teaspoon chilli sauce

1 teaspoon salt

2 tablespoons water

½ cup (125 g) sugar

½ cup (125 ml) vinegar

1 Place plums and apricots in a wok. Add chilli sauce, salt and water. Bring to the boil and simmer gently 15 minutes. Add a little more water if the mixture becomes too dry.
2 Stir in sugar and vinegar and simmer 20 to 30 minutes until the sauce reaches a chutney-like consistency. Pour sauce into a sterilised jar, cover and refrigerate when cool. This sauce will keep several months.

MAKES ABOUT 1 CUP (250 ML)

Top row left to right: Pepper and Salt Mix in mortar and pestle, and in jar, Ginger Soy Dip; bottom row left to right: Plum Sauce, Sherry Soy Dip, Sweet and Sour Sauce, Sweet and Sour Ginger Sauce

SWEET AND SOUR FRUITY SAUCE

½ cup (125 g) sugar

½ cup (125 ml) vinegar

2 tablespoons soy sauce

2 tablespoons sherry

3 tablespoons tomato sauce

2 tablespoons cornflour blended with ½ cup pineapple juice

1 In a saucepan, combine sugar, vinegar, soy sauce, sherry and tomato sauce. Bring to the boil and add blended cornflour and pineapple juice, stirring constantly until the sauce is thickened.

MAKES ABOUT 1½ CUPS (375 ML)

SWEET AND SOUR SAUCE

½ cup (125 g) sugar

½ cup (125 ml) vinegar

4 to 5 tablespoons light soy sauce

1 tablespoon dark soy sauce (optional)

2 tablespoons sherry

1½ tablespoons cornflour blended with ½ cup (125 ml) water

1 In a saucepan, combine sugar, vinegar, light soy sauce, dark soy sauce and sherry. Bring to the boil and stir in the blended cornflour and water to thicken.

MAKES ABOUT 1½ CUPS (375 ML)

GINGER-SOY DIP

2 tablespoons oil

1 tablespoon finely chopped spring onions, white part only

½ teaspoon finely grated fresh ginger root

4 tablespoons soy sauce

1 Heat oil in a wok. Add spring onions and ginger root and stir-fry 30 seconds. Add soy sauce and remove from heat.

MAKES ABOUT ⅔ CUP (160 ML)

DESSERTS

The Chinese very rarely eat desserts and most are
reserved for banquets, formal dinners or are made for one of the many
festivals that the Chinese celebrate.

Fresh fruit in season is a good choice for people who
like to finish a meal with something sweet. Fortune cookies are always
baked commercially and are available, in packets, from Chinese specialty
shops. Moon cakes, which are also available from shops, are never prepared
at home as they are time consuming and require a long list of
unusual ingredients. The cakes are filled with a lightly sweetened,
rich-red soybean paste and are exchanged as gifts at
the Moon Festival, during September.

Fruit ices would be another suitable dessert for a Chinese meal.
Marco Polo was introduced to these on his voyage to China and brought
the idea back to the Western world.

Mandarin Sorbet (page 90) and Lychee
and Ginger Mousse (page 91)

Toffee Apples

TOFFEE APPLES

4 ripe apples

1 egg

1 egg white

2 tablespoons plain flour

**2 tablespoons cornflour oil,
for deep frying**

¼ cup (60 ml) vegetable oil

¼ cup (60 g) sugar

¼ cup (90 g) honey

**1½ tablespoons white sesame seeds
(optional)**

1 bowl iced water

1 Peel and core apples and cut each apple in six to eight wedges. Beat egg and egg white together and fold in sifted flour and cornflour to make a batter.

2 Heat oil for deep-frying. Dip apple wedges in batter and deep-fry until golden. Remove and drain on absorbent kitchen paper.

3 In a saucepan heat vegetable oil, add sugar and heat, stirring constantly, until sugar dissolves. Stir in honey.

4 Coat apple fritters with syrup and sprinkle with sesame seeds.

5 Serve while piping hot. Let each guest dip apple fritters into iced water. This will cause the syrup coating to harden so the fritters will be crisp and crackling on the outside.

NOTE: Toffee apples can be prepared to the stage of dipping in the syrup.

SERVES 4

MANDARIN SORBET

500 g mandarins

1¼ cups (250 g) caster sugar

1¾ cups (450 ml) water

2 egg whites

1 Peel mandarins. Using a teaspoon, scrape the underside of the skin to remove any white pith from the zest. Cut the zest into thin strips. Combine zest, sugar and water in a saucepan. Heat until sugar completely dissolves. Raise heat and boil syrup for 5 minutes. Remove from heat and cool completely.

2 Squeeze juice from mandarins and strain. Strain syrup and combine with mandarin juice. Freeze mixture until partially frozen, stirring occasionally.

3 Whisk egg whites until stiff. Beat into soft ice mixture. Freeze until ice is firmer. Whisk again until smooth. Return to freezer until firm. Remove with small ice cream scoop.

SERVES 4 TO 6

LYCHEE AND GINGER MOUSSE

400 g canned lychees, drained (reserve 2 tablespoons juice)

1 tablespoon ginger in syrup, drained and chopped (reserve 1 tablespoon syrup)

2 teaspoons gelatine

300 ml thickened cream, whipped

3 egg whites, beaten

1 Chop most of the lychees with ginger. Place gelatine in a heatproof bowl, add reserved lychee juice and dissolve over hot water.

2 Lightly fold cream into egg whites. Add lychee mixture, reserved ginger syrup and gelatine, until well combined.

3 Pour into six individual glasses and refrigerate until set. Top with remaining fruit and rosettes of cream.

4 Alternatively, the mixture can be set in a wetted ring mould and served whole, garnished with extra fruit and cream.

SERVES 4 TO 6

ALMOND FLOAT

2½ cups (625 ml) milk

¼ cup (60 g) sugar

almond essence

1½ tablespoons gelatine

½ cup (125 ml) water

selection of prepared fresh fruit

canned lychees

1 Scald milk, remove from heat and add sugar. Cool slightly then add almond essence; cool. Sprinkle gelatine over water and leave until water is absorbed. Dissolve gelatine over hot water and cool. Stir into milk mixture.

2 When ready to serve, cut almond gelatine into diamond shapes. Place fruit in a serving bowl and arrange diamond shapes on top.

SERVES 4

RAMBUTAN COCKTAIL

565 g canned rambutan fruit, drained

400 g honeydew melon balls

400 g rockmelon balls

1 tablespoon orange liqueur

1 egg white

¼ cup (50 g) caster sugar mixed with a few drops green food colouring

chilled sparkling white wine

1 Combine fruit and liqueur. Place egg white and sugar on two separate plates.

2 Invert six dessert glasses and dip rim into egg white, then into coloured sugar. Fill glasses with assorted fruit and liqueur. Cover with sparkling wine. Serve chilled.

NOTE: Rambutan is a bright red fruit, oval in shape, which comes from Malaysia. It is available fresh or canned at supermarkets. If you need to substitute, you can use lychees or mangosteen.

SERVES 4 TO 6

❖ **FRUITS**

Many oriental fruits are available canned and can be served individually with ice cream or combine several for a fruit salad. The most popular are lychees, longans, rambutan, mangosteen, mandarin quarters and jackfruit.

Almond Float

SNOW BALLS

2 cups (250 g) glutinous rice flour

¼ cup (60 g) cornflour

2 tablespoons caster sugar

1 tablespoon lard

¾ cup (180 ml) water

85 g red bean paste

60 g cashew nuts, chopped

2 cups (190 g) desiccated coconut

cherries or strawberries, to garnish (190 g)

1 Combine rice and cornflour with sugar. Rub in lard, add water and stir with a knife to form a dough. Knead 2 to 3 minutes. Roll dough into a sausage shape and divide into 16 pieces. Shape into balls.

2 Combine bean paste and cashew nuts. Divide into 16 portions. Make an indentation or hollow in each dough ball. Fill each with paste mixture, draw edges together to enclose filling. Reshape into a ball.

3 Cook in boiling water 8 minutes, stirring gently to prevent sticking on bottom of saucepan. Remove balls with a strainer. Cool slightly, then roll in coconut. Decorate each with half a cherry or strawberry. Store at room temperature.

VARIATION: 1 cup of coconut can be lightly toasted. Roll half the balls in each cup coconut.

SERVES 4 TO 6

FRESH FRUIT ROLLS

1 firm ripe mango, peeled and cut in 2 cm dice

3 slices ripe fresh pineapple, peeled and cut in 2 cm dice

1 large apple, peeled and cut in 2 cm dice

3 kiwi fruit, peeled and cut in 2 cm dice

3 firm bananas, peeled and cut in 2 cm dice

200 g strawberries

3 teaspoons orange liqueur

6 to 8 large spring roll skins

1 egg white, beaten

vegetable oil, for frying

icing sugar

vanilla ice cream

1 Combine fruit in a bowl. Sprinkle with liqueur and stand 15 minutes; drain. Divide fruit between spring roll skins. Brush edges with egg white. Roll up as for ordinary spring rolls.

2 Fry three rolls at a time in oil to cover. When golden, remove and drain well.

3 Dust with icing sugar and serve with ice cream.

SERVES 6 TO 8

FRIED FRUIT BON BONS

100 g dried apricots, finely chopped

100 g dates, finely chopped

50 g crystallised ginger, finely chopped

90 g pecan nuts or cashews, chopped

1½ teaspoons chopped orange zest

3 teaspoons orange liqueur or orange juice

200 g wonton skins

vegetable oil, for frying

icing sugar

1 Combine apricots, dates, ginger, pecans, orange zest and liqueur. Roll a tablespoon of filling in hands until 2.5 x 0.8 cm in diameter.

2 Place filling across wonton wrapper. Moisten edges with water. Roll up to seal, twisting ends.

3 Fry bon bons in oil to cover until crisp. Drain well. Dust with icing sugar and serve with Chinese tea.

SERVES 4 TO 6

ASSORTED FRUIT FRITTERS

1 large firm mango, peeled

4 firm bananas, peeled

4 slices fresh pineapple

plain flour, for dusting

¼ teaspoon cinnamon

BATTER

2 cups (250 g) plain flour

1 teaspoon baking powder

¼ teaspoon salt

⅔ cup (160 ml) milk

⅔ cup (160 ml) cold water

vegetable oil, for deep-frying

icing sugar

1 Cut fruit into serving pieces. Combine flour and cinnamon and lightly coat fruit.

2 TO MAKE BATTER: Sift flour, baking powder and salt into a bowl. Combine milk and water, and beat into flour to form a smooth batter. Strain before using.

3 Dip fruit into batter and fry in hot oil to cover until golden. Drain well. Arrange on serving platter. Sprinkle with icing sugar.

SERVES 6 TO 8

MONGOLIAN RICE PUDDING

4 tablespoons brown rice

1 cup (250 ml) water

2½ cups (625 ml) milk or soy milk

½ cup (125 g) sugar

½ cup (60 g) walnuts, coarsely chopped

¼ cup (40 g) raisins

cinnamon or nutmeg

1 Put rice and water in a saucepan. Cook until water has been absorbed. Add milk and sugar and cook over low heat until mixture thickens. Add walnuts and raisins.

2 Serve hot, sprinkled with cinnamon.

SERVES 6

ALMOND AND CASHEW NUT COOKIES

1 cup (250 g) lard

1 cup (220 g) caster sugar

1 egg, beaten

2 tablespoons ground almonds

2 tablespoons ground cashew nuts

½ teaspoon vanilla

½ teaspoon almond essence

2½ cups (310 g) plain flour

1½ level teaspoons baking powder

pinch salt

1 Cream lard and sugar together in a bowl. Add egg, almonds, cashews, vanilla and almond essence.

2 Sift flour, baking powder and salt together. Fold into creamed mixture and knead lightly. Shape dough into walnut-sized balls. Arrange on lightly greased trays. Press each ball to flatten slightly with a fork.

3 Bake at 200°C (400°F) until pale golden, 15 to 20 minutes.

MAKES ABOUT 24

❖ **HINT**

When deep-frying food, only add small quantities of ingredients to the oil at one time. This maintains the oil's temperature and prevents absorption.

Almond and Cashew Nut Cookies

MEASURING MADE EASY

HOW TO MEASURE DRY INGREDIENTS

15 g	½ oz	
30 g	1 oz	
60 g	2 oz	
90 g	3 oz	
125 g	4 oz	(¼ lb)
155 g	5 oz	
185 g	6 oz	
220 g	7 oz	
250 g	8 oz	(½ lb)
280 g	9 oz	
315 g	10 oz	
345 g	11 oz	
375 g	12 oz	(¾ lb)
410 g	13 oz	
440 g	14 oz	
470 g	15 oz	
500 g	16 oz	(1 lb)
750 g	24 oz	(1½ lb)
1 kg	32 oz	(2 lb)

QUICK CONVERSIONS

5 mm	¼ inch	
1 cm	½ inch	
2 cm	¾ inch	
2.5 cm	1 inch	
5 cm	2 inches	
6 cm	2½ inches	
8 cm	3 inches	
10 cm	4 inches	
12 cm	5 inches	
15 cm	6 inches	
18 cm	7 inches	
20 cm	8 inches	
23 cm	9 inches	
25 cm	10 inches	
28 cm	11 inches	
30 cm	12 inches	(1 foot)
46 cm	18 inches	
50 cm	20 inches	
61 cm	24 inches	(2 feet)
77 cm	30 inches	

NOTE: We developed the recipes in this book in Australia where the tablespoon measure is 20 ml. In many other countries the tablespoon is 15 ml. For most recipes this difference will not be noticeable.

However, for recipes using baking powder, gelatine, bicarbonate of soda, small amounts of flour and cornflour, we suggest you add an extra teaspoon for each tablespoon specified.

Many people find it very convenient to use cup measurements. You can buy special measuring cups or measure water in an ordinary household cup to check it holds 250 ml (8 fl oz). This can then be used for both liquid and dry cup measurements.

MEASURING LIQUIDS

METRIC CUPS

¼ cup	60 ml	2 fluid ounces
⅓ cup	80 ml	2½ fluid ounces
½ cup	125 ml	4 fluid ounces
¾ cup	180 ml	6 fluid ounces
1 cup	250 ml	8 fluid ounces

METRIC SPOONS

¼ teaspoon	1.25 ml
½ teaspoon	2.5 ml
1 teaspoon	5 ml
1 tablespoon	20 ml

OVEN TEMPERATURES

TEMPERATURES	CELSIUS (°C)	FAHRENHEIT (°F)	GAS MARK
Very Slow	120	250	½
Slow	150	300	2
Moderate	160-180	325-350	3-4
Moderately hot	190-200	375-400	5-6
Hot	220-230	425-450	7-8
Very hot	250-260	475-500	9-10

Published by Murdoch Books®,
a division of Murdoch Magazines Pty Limited,
213 Miller Street, North Sydney NSW 2060.

Cover photograph by Ashley Mackevicius, styled by Wendy Berecry.
Murdoch Books® Associate Food Editors: Kerrie Ray, Tracy Rutherford.
Publisher: Anne Wilson. Publishing Manager: Catie Ziller.
Production Coordinator: Liz Fitzgerald. Managing Editor:
Susan Tomnay. Creative Director: Marylouise Brammer.
International Manager: Mark Newman. Marketing Manager:
Mark Smith. National Sales Manager: Karon McGrath.
Photo Librarian: Dianne Bedford.

National Library of Australia Cataloguing-in-Publication Data: Chinese cooking made easy. Includes index. ISBN 0 86411 513 X. 1. Cookery, Chinese. I. Marsland, Douglas. (Series: Bay Books cookery collection.) 641.5951. First published in Australia in 1989. This edition 1996. Printed by Griffin Press, Adelaide.

Copyright© Text, design, photography and illustrations Murdoch Books®.

INDEX